<u>**OVERVIEW**</u>

Complaining is an epidemic that has plagued society ever since we can remember. The facts show that the average person complains 30 times every day. Considering we only have an average of 27 conversations per day, that is an eye-opening number. Simply put, complaining can be a relatable topic for every person on this planet.

This book dives into various facts, stories, and situations throughout the author's life that can be learning moments for the reader. Why live a life filled with negativity and complaints when we can train our mind to eliminate or at the very least minimize our pessimism? Every person has the ability to train their brain and alter their mindset in order to be happier.

The author creates types of complainers that we all know or maybe that we are. We want to grab the attention of the reader and help people realize how prevalent complaining is in their lives and teach them how to make a change.

<u>*Introduction*</u>

If you asked me five years ago to try and write a book, I would have complained that it was too hard. I would have complained that it would take too long. I would have complained that my life wasn't extraordinary enough anyway.

But then in 2018, I just shut up and wrote a book. It *was* hard. It *did* take a long time. My life *still isn't* extraordinary. But after I put those complaints to rest, there were a few situations that arose in my life that helped me find the internal drive to complete the task. All that was left was the reality that I *could* write a book. So I did.

That is the debilitating power of complaining. It can take seeds of potential and squash them before they even hit the soil. The fact of the matter is that it is easier to complain than take action.

About two years ago, after a series of events you will soon learn about, I realized how many complainers I had to deal with in my life. Even worse, I saw that I was one of them. It might seem cliché, but that realization made me open my eyes.

I don't have a PhD in Psychology, but what I have is a lifetime worth of experience with complaining and with complainers. Throughout this book, you'll read several stories and facts about positivity, negativity, mindset, and happiness. These topics have been researched for decades by men and women much smarter than me, but I'm not going to spend the next 100+ pages complaining about my intelligence -- I'm going to learn, and I'm going to share that knowledge with you.

Hopefully while reading this book, some of these stories will resonate with you. At the very least, I hope some of the facts will bring new awareness into your life.

Most people would agree that, as a society, we latch on to negativity. It can get tiring. Just watch the nightly news for five minutes and see what it does to your body language. But we don't have to do this anymore.

There are several ways to train yourself to turn your thoughts away from the negative. The goal of this book is to help those of you who feel you use complaining as a crutch. So check your posture, turn the page, and let's choose to be happy.

CHAPTER 1: Who is This Guy?

College baseball coaching jobs are extremely competitive and difficult to land. In 2014, I was on a cross country road trip when my old college coach, Ed Sprague, and I ran into each other. He asked me why I hadn't applied for the coaching vacancy at my alma mater, the University of the Pacific. I told him I would definitely be interested and I continued on my road trip. I was coaching High School baseball and scouting part-time for the Baltimore Orioles, but moving to the college ranks was my ultimate goal. I'll never forget driving across the northern part of the United States through some of the most beautiful mountains I've seen and receiving a call from Coach Sprague. He was a man of few words, he simply asked, "You want it?" Of course, I accepted. I was 26-years old and a full-time paid assistant coach with a salary and benefits. There weren't many coaches that were full-time in their mid-20's at the Division-I level at that time.

After only three months on the job, I knew this is what I wanted to be doing. I loved every aspect of my daily duties. The relationships that I was building with the players was my favorite job attribute. I also enjoyed recruiting, which was a major part of what I did.

I had met a girl in my first few weeks at UOP. We had a lot in common, however, we were both dating other people at the time. We enjoyed each other's company in group settings for a while until our friendship blossomed into more. Her name was Julie and she was too good to be true. The script of my life was being directed perfectly.

Then, just as I had gotten a year under my belt at Pacific, disaster struck. I called Coach Sprague to ask him about coming to campus to visit with a recruit on a Saturday. His response, "I can't make it Joe. I can't give you the details now, but I won't be able to make it." His tone was one of extreme disappointment. I knew something was up, so I called our other assistant coach (we called him Snacks) and he told me there were some compliance and NCAA rules that our baseball program had allegedly broken. I anxiously waited for the next few days to hear any news about what had happened. I complained to Julie about how everything was being kept from me. I felt that I had a right to know what was going on.

After only one season, with a young team and me still learning the ropes in the college baseball world, our entire coaching staff was let go. More selfishly, only 10 months into my dream job and dream girl, I was back where I started. I spent the Summer wondering why this happened and how unfair it was. There was a vacancy down the road from my old high school at the University of San Diego that I didn't get. I had a phone interview with San Jose State University, but could not land the job. Every school looking to fill roles seemed to want more experienced coaches. How could I acquire that experience if nobody would hire me? Towards the end of the Summer, Mark Martinez (Head Coach at San Diego State) called and expressed an interest in me for their Volunteer Coaching role.

A volunteer?! How could I go from a full-time role down to a volunteer role? I felt that the world owed me more because I had spent my entire life pouring everything I had into baseball. There was a fork in the road. Was I going to take the road where everything I do is half-assed because I felt like I've been screwed? At the time that sounded pretty good to me. Or should I take the high road and work hard with the realization that San Diego State could be a great opportunity for me. I felt bad for myself and I wanted everyone else in my life to feel bad for me too...the problem was that nobody did.

After a couple months of soul searching, Mark Martinez offered me the job and brought me on as the Volunteer Coach. I began working at San Diego State in August of 2015. I spent my first year at San Diego State as 'The Complainer'. It's not that I didn't work hard – I did the entire year – but I carried my best friend, negativity, around with me at all times.

I complained daily to anybody who would listen. However, looking back, I now see that I had a choice to flip my thought process and see things from a more positive point of view. For example, here's a list of complaints I had versus ways I could have flipped my mindset and turned them into positive thoughts:

-I'm too knowledgeable to be a volunteer vs. I have a plethora of knowledge, but I'm young and can always learn more and become a better coach
-I can barely afford my bills vs. How can I make a little more money so I don't stress about it?
-I work 10-12 hour days and don't get any credit vs. I am accomplishing so much throughout my day and helping so many athletes

I felt bad for myself and was so negative that it dragged people around me down. My normally happy and upbeat then-girlfriend (now wife), Julie, would slump her shoulders when we would see each other, knowing to expect another story about my shitty day. I didn't even realize how grateful I should be that Julie moved from Northern California down to San Diego a few weeks before I was let go at UOP for a job opportunity of her own! Selfishly, I would get to my tiny bedroom in my friend's condo, call Julie if we were not together, and give her all of the details about how awful my day was. I did not even consider Julie's feelings or that she might be tired; I only cared that I was miserable, and she needed to be my sounding board for my daily whining sessions.

I'm glad I met her at UOP in 2014, because there's no way she would have fallen in love with the moping, delusional version of Joey I was my first year at SDSU. At UOP, I was fun to be around because I enjoyed my job and living situation. I enjoyed what I did and who I spent time with. I didn't have problems or have to overcome any adversity. Once our coaching staff was let go at UOP, I was hit with a whirlwind of emotions, mostly negativity. I don't know why Julie stuck it out with me when I was at San Diego State; I was a compulsive complainer. I thought that my life was in the dumps because that's what I trained my brain to believe. I still had a great life, a great job, and a great girlfriend. I just couldn't see the positive through all of the negative. I can't imagine how tiring it was for Julie to listen to me every day. If she wasn't as patient of a person as she is, she probably would have told me to kick rocks.

After a losing season at San Diego State, I was once again looking for jobs all over the country. No way I was going back to SDSU for another year of $0 and working my ass off. I didn't want to burn through my savings and my pride. That Summer was a turning point for me. In August of 2016, Head Coach Mark Martinez called me into his office to have a talk.

When Mark Martinez calls you into the office and asks you to close the door, you can count on the conversation being one of significant importance. It is common practice in college sports for coaches to call the head coach at a school if they have an interest in an assistant they may want to hire. I went into the office expecting Coach Martinez to tell me that a coach had contacted him about hiring me full-time at another university. I was excited to say the least.

I walked in, closed the door at his request, and sat down on the couch while Coach Martinez was at his desk. I was immediately shell-shocked after hearing the first words out of his mouth. "I am going to get to the point Joey, I am thinking about letting you go." All I could think was, "Am I at the point in my life where I am going to get fired from a volunteer job? They don't even pay me!"

I responded to Coach Martinez in a defensive manner, "I think it was a bad year for everyone. I know that I can bring more to help the team this coming season. You won't have to worry about my commitment to the Aztecs at all." He replied, "If this is going to work, I need more positive energy and a willingness to do more. You need to be 100% bought in to what we are doing."

My mind immediately shifted to complaining mode. He was not there to see all of the extra hours I put in every day giving lessons to kids and coaching youth travel baseball in order to pay my rent. I thought to myself, "I worked harder than everyone!"

At this point, I knew I was in survival mode and needed to say something that he wanted to hear. "I will definitely bring a more positive vibe to the field every day and do whatever you need."

The fact that Coach Martinez was thinking of firing me was like a slap in the face, but he was right in considering that option. I spent every day complaining and whining about how everything in my life was unfair. Luckily, after that meeting he decided to keep me around for another year.

From that point on, I told myself that I was going to work as hard as I can in everything that I do. Spending my days complaining was tiring; not to mention how miserable I was to be around for my friends and family. I started to get on a better routine in the mornings and have my days mapped out so there were no surprises. When you have a better plan in the morning of what your day will look like, you are less likely to get blindsided. I consciously thought about my days before they happened and visualized happiness and positivity. I attacked every task with passion and excitement. 2016-17 was a blast and I made it a point to be a more enjoyable person to spend time with. I would get up in the morning at 5:30am and have a good workout in San Diego State's amazing weight room (it had been completely remodeled that Summer). I would then have a healthy breakfast and head up to the office before everyone would get there. I would have about an hour of work done before any of the other coaches would get there. This enabled me to get some work of my own finished before other things would pop up. When Coach Martinez would arrive, all of the coaches would meet in his office and get the plan for the day. This was good for me because I could then design my day based on the program's needs. Around 12:30pm, I would usually head down to the field, eat lunch, then set up practice. After practice was done around 4:00pm, I would stay at school and give lessons or go coach a youth baseball practice until 7:00 or 8:00 at night.

These were long days that I had. When I went to sleep at night I knew what to expect the following day and when I woke up in the morning I forced myself to be excited for the day even when I wasn't 100% energetic about it. The positivity I had was seemingly contagious, and while it may not have caused better opportunities, it's hard for me to separate the way I was acting from what was about to come in my life. My relationship with Julie was getting stronger and the Aztecs were getting better. Most importantly, the lack of complaining had a direct effect on me: *it made me happier*.

After the Aztecs made it to an NCAA regional, in the Summer of 2017, my phone rang. It was a number I didn't recognize, but I'm glad I decided to answer it. On the other end was Ryan Garko, a former Major League Baseball player and the new Head Coach at my alma mater, UOP. He was brief but clear: he wanted to interview me for his Pitching Coach vacancy. He was in Phoenix at the time he was hired and had just started moving his family up to Northern California. I wanted to interview but we were having trouble finding a time and place to get it done. I told him I would be in Phoenix the next day to meet with him. It was only about a 5 ½ hour drive to get there. I wanted the job so I took matters into my own hands and drove out to meet him. He seemed to like the fact that I was motivated and excited about the position. Things started looking up once again. I don't know if it was a direct correlation, but my positive outlook on life led to another great opportunity.

Ryan Garko offered me the job a week after the interview.

Complaining has been a human attribute forever. I don't have any proof, but I imagine that before words were spoken, complaining was done using noises and bad body language. I'd like to go back to the stone age and watch our early ancestors groaning at each other after the wind blew out their precious fire. Complaining might feel good in the moment -- it's great for getting attention -- but nobody that I've ever met enjoys being the sounding board for someone that gripes too often.

To be fair, we all have things in our lives to complain about. There have been two key points in my life that I remember vividly and realized that I needed to make a change. There is also a third story that I'll go over in this chapter about a 5th grade project. It wasn't eye-opening at the time, but looking back now, I realize how valuable the lesson that I learned was. In all of these cases, I eventually realized that a changed perspective could only help me. But without these situations, I am unsure if I would have ever had a revelation that I could be different.

As a life-long athlete, I've learned that sports are a great example of where to find complainers. If you told me that you watched a baseball, basketball, football, or soccer game and none of the players went "palms up" (a gesture made with opened palms raised in a supinated position non-verbally expressing begging or complaining) because the referee or umpire missed a call, I'd laugh.

Most complaining comes from people wanting attention or sympathy. Complaining doesn't improve any situation. Just as people want praise for their successes in life, they also want consolation for their failures.

But what are these complaints really saying?

I lost...*feel bad for me*
I'm hurt...*feel bad for me*
I failed...*feel bad for me*
The umpire made a bad call...*feel bad for me*

Growing up as a baseball player, I think every time I struck out from age 8-22, I blamed the umpire. "How could someone as perfect as me possibly make a mistake like that? And if coaches told me the umpire was right, then they must have missed it, too. How could everyone be so blind?!" Athletes and sports are great, but watching them whine about everything that doesn't go their way can get irritating. The good news is that with some work you can minimize complaining and upgrade your life immensely.

I'll never forget a project that my classmates and I were able to do in Mrs. Reeves' 5th grade class at Paloma Elementary School. We had been learning about various rainforests, which didn't interest me as much as reading about wars or world leaders, but it still interested me. I walked into Mrs. Reeves' colorful classroom where the walls were filled with pictures and artwork ready to learn about the rainforest for our final lesson of the chapter.

When we sat down at our desks, we all had outlined drawings of the rainforest and dozens of colored pencils and markers. Mrs. Reeves didn't give us much direction other than color it and make it look as nice as possible; we would be graded on the assignment. The task seemed pretty simple (although my art skills could be compared to a blind monkey). We took our time coloring these vibrant trees, plants, and animals. After an hour, it was time for recess.

When we came back from recess, we all walked around and looked at each other's work. I felt proud of what I had created and thought it was one of the better ones in the class. My favorite piece of art was done by the girl sitting directly next to me, Eliza. The way that she was able to utilize various shades of greens in the trees made them pop. Her animals blended in with the backgrounds as if they were hiding from me as I looked down at the paper. When we sat back down, Mrs. Reeves handed out black sharpies to everyone in the class. The next simple direction from Mrs. Reeves was, "Scribble out everything that you just did."

I was frustrated because I had truly taken my time and done great work! Most of my classmates began to look at each other and complain about the fact that they had to destroy their work. Some of the kids even told Mrs. Reeves that this wasn't fair. Most of us were tentative and didn't want to start this process because of the time and effort that we had put in before recess. Plus, something as beautiful as Eliza's should be framed, not ruined.

The point of the exercise was that Mrs. Reeves wanted to show us what was happening to our rainforests. Companies were cutting down trees at a record rate and she wanted us to feel sorry for ourselves for destroying the work that we had done. God only knows how long the rainforests have been growing and developing for, and we had companies ruining millions of years of growth in a matter of days.

Something that I learned much later in life came in that moment from Eliza. While all of us protested, Eliza -- like a Buddhist monk wiping away an intricate mandala -- very calmly scribbled the black sharpie from top to bottom as if she weren't affected. The beautiful trees, the vibrant raindrops, the sweet monkey -- all were replaced by a sea of black.

But then, after everyone kept complaining to Mrs. Reeves, Eliza walked up to her desk and asked for another blank slate. She spent lunch that day coloring another rainforest -- even better than the first one.

She could have complained like everyone else in the class, instead she realized that she had another opportunity to make a masterpiece. Eliza couldn't control the assignment that Mrs. Reeves gave us, but she could control how to handle it in a positive way. Her reaction was minimal and she found a way to limit her frustration with the project and complete a new drawing. It was something that I didn't notice at the time as important; but looking back, Eliza never complained and always seemed to carry a smile on her face; no matter what 5th grade drama she may have encountered.

Chapter 2: Facts About Complaining

Studies show that the average person complains 30 times every day (Laura Marham, Active Family Magazine). It's hard for me to put into context just how many complaints that is, but I'll try. According to newswiretoday, the average person has 27 conversations in a day. That would put us at over 1 complaint per conversation. That seems insane to me! If you live until you're 85 years old, that will put you hovering around 1,000,000 complaints throughout your lifetime. This means that you've spent 1,000,000+ minutes or almost 700 days of your life (the only one that you will get) complaining. In my non-professional opinion, we can do a much better job of being resourceful and using those precious minutes more wisely.

"Every time you complain, your irritability — like a virus — is neurologically picked up by every person who hears your voice or sees your face. So, by all means, train your brain to be optimistic and positive because (according to 30+ years of longitudinal research conducted by Duke University and the Mayo Clinic), it will literally add years to your life." —Mark Waldman

Mark Waldman makes a great point – to make it as simple as possible, if you're negative, people don't want to be around you. If you are optimistic, you will attract other positive people. What is the point of living if we're going to complain and attract negative attention to ourselves? Happier people live longer and more fulfilled lives. There are endless facts and figures that correlate negativity to complaining and correlate complaining to a less enjoyable life. A great goal for everyone (for obvious reasons) is to be happy in life. If we have a negative virus following us around in our daily lives because we have to whine about every obstacle we face, it is going to be a long and bumpy road to our graves.

Reading and studying about the human brain has opened up a new outlook for me into how we think and attack every day thoughts and tasks. The famous quote from Donald Hebb, "Cells that fire together, wire together" holds true in everything we do in life. The brain has a collection of synapses separated by a small gap called the synaptic cleft. Your brain shoots a chemical across the synaptic cleft from synapse to synapse to transfer information. Each time this happens, the synapse gets closer together literally rewiring the brain. Basically, the more you do something, the closer the synapses get. This is why the more we do something, the less foreign it feels to us (i.e. riding a bike).

For me, I relate this to baseball because that is what I've been doing my entire life. My synapses are completed wired together in regards to throwing a ball. When I was young and learning how to throw different pitches and manipulate the ball in my hand, the synapses were still working on closing the gap. Now, whenever I grab a baseball to play catch, I don't think about anything. My brain knows exactly what my body has to do to efficiently get the ball from point A to point B. Even as I'm typing this, I don't think about where the keys on this keyboard are at, my brain just knows from several years of memorization and practice. I've typed thousands of pages throughout my life and the synapses have grown close.

A leader in his field of study that I've really grown fond of over the past several months is Dr. Joe Dispenza. He is a neuroscientist that has an amazing backstory that has led to his passion for the mind over body connection. After listening to and reading several of Dr. Dispenza's interviews, articles, and books, the most important lesson that I've taken from his unbelievable amount of information is that we need to be aware of our unconscious behaviors and thoughts. If we can be aware of the thoughts that we don't want to have, we can catch them before we act on them.

In sports, visualization has become more and more popular throughout the years. I try to have my players do some visualization training at least three times a week. Seeing situations arise in your brain and having success in those situations gives an athlete a mental edge. If we can rehearse these situations in baseball, why can't we rehearse these situations in real life? The short answer is, we can. If we close our eyes and train our brains to catch ourselves when we have a negative thought, we can see through our own eyes how to better react to that situation the next time it arises. I started doing this in my life with aspects that I wanted to improve on and have found some interesting results.

I started with something small, like the weather. I've always been a huge complainer about the cold (I'm from San Diego). Instead of complaining about it not being 72 degrees and sunny every day, I started visualizing myself standing in the dugout at UOP's home field and it being 35 degrees. I've felt in these visualization sessions that 35 degrees feels normal. My body doesn't know that my brain is taking over in these instances. "The brain does not know the difference between what you're imagining and what you're experiencing." Dr. Dispenza discusses in depth how we need to teach our body that our mind is in control. If we don't react to a problem, we are not giving power to it. This is how we train our brains to overcome various negative situations or thoughts in our daily lives.

Reacting to our problems or situations that occur in our lives is natural. We all react, but how long we react is really the bigger problem. Imagine this, you take your son to the grocery store and he sees a fruit roll-up and asks, "Mom, can I have this?" You respond with a basic, "No you may not." The situation could be over without any other speed bumps; or, the child can start screaming, crying, and *reacting negatively* to the situation. "Cognitive behavioral therapy (CBT) is a psychotherapy that is based on the cognitive model: the way that individuals perceive a situation is more closely connected to their reaction than the situation itself." (Aaron Beck) This idea is nothing new to us. Aaron Beck is a world-renowned psychiatrist and is regarded as the Father of cognitive therapy. He has been studying CBT since the 1940's but really dove into his own research in the 50's. "Individuals' perceptions are often distorted and dysfunctional when they are distressed. They can learn to identify and evaluate their "automatic thoughts" (spontaneously occurring verbal or imaginal cognitions), and to correct their thinking so that it more closely resembles reality. When they do so, their distress usually decreases, they are able to behave more functionally, and (especially in anxiety cases), their physiological arousal abates." (Aaron Beck) These quotes above have a strong relationship to the idea of reacting. Training our brain to consciously change our negative "automatic thoughts" is a tall order. When we are able to do that, our anxiety and stress decrease which allows us to be happier.

As I sit down and type this, I had something happen yesterday that could have caused a large-scale reaction. It was a normal day, I got home from work at the same time as my wife and we walked in the house together. She peeked her head outside and noticed that we should have had packages delivered, but there weren't any there. As I looked through our security footage, I found a man get out of a Chevy Tahoe, walk up to our front door, and take all of our packages. As frustrating as this is, I am grateful that I am not in a situation where I need to steal. I can either let this continue to annoy me and complain about it to friends and family, or I can find a solution to the problem. I filed a police report and we will have future packages dropped over our side fence now, which is locked. Problem solved. Julie and I handled this the best way we could without letting our reaction last for hours or days.

There have been several studies done about how many thoughts a day we have and how many of those thoughts are repetitive. It's safe to say that we have around 60,000+ thoughts a day and 90% of them are recurring thoughts that we have daily. If you have a negative mindset and regularly dwell on the past, this is a statistic that you should keep in your memory bank. Your brain is a device that records all of the moments throughout your life. If you have had 90% negative thoughts, living in the past with those thoughts is not going to be beneficial for you. Making a commitment to look towards the future and change that thought process is the only way to start eliminating the negativity in your life. Having trips, weddings or events to look forward to help you enjoy the present moment. If we have nothing to look forward to, it can be difficult to enjoy your present state. When those future moments arrive, embrace them!

That change of mindset is going to take a lot of work and feel extremely uncomfortable at times, but I guarantee it will have a positive effect. Dr. Dispenza talks about the idea of something feeling right vs. something feeling familiar. The change that you make might not feel right at the onset, and you'll want to go back to what feels familiar. This is why you must commit to the change and be aware of those negative thoughts as they enter your brain.

I can write an entire book on Dr. Dispenza's studies and experiences, but I'll stop there. He has several books and interviews that I recommend for anyone that is looking to find ways to turn their lives from negative to positive.

"Your thoughts reshape your brain, and thus are changing a physical construct of reality." –Steven Parton

Your thoughts literally reshape your brain! According to Dr. Joseph Mercola, as time goes by, science provides more and more evidence that your brain is malleable and continually changing in response to your lifestyle, physiology, and environment.

"Repeated complaining rewires your brain to make future complaining more likely. Over time, you find it's easier to be negative than to be positive, regardless of what's happening around you. Complaining becomes your default behavior, which changes how people perceive you." –Travis Bradberry (Cofounder of TalentSmart, emotional intelligence tests and training)

Let me repeat that, if we continually complain throughout our lifetimes, our brain is rewiring itself to make that our norm. Just like brushing your teeth when you wake up in the morning or pouring yourself a coffee, you don't have to think about how to do those things because they have become natural to you. Complaining can be our default when we enter into a conversation if that's what we have grown accustomed to. Now imagine if your default was positivity and happiness. Do you think you'd be more enjoyable to be around for friends and family? Luckily, I learned this before it got out of hand in my life. I was playing with that fine line of negativity when I had an epiphany at San Diego State.

People that complain more, stress more. "The stress hormone, cortisol, is public health enemy number one. Scientists have known for years that elevated cortisol levels: interfere with learning and memory, lower immune function and bone density, increase weight gain, blood pressure, cholesterol, heart disease...The list goes on and on. Chronic stress and elevated cortisol levels also increase risk for depression, mental illness, and lower life expectancy. This week, two separate studies were published in Science linking elevated cortisol levels as a potential trigger for mental illness and decreased resilience—especially in adolescence. Cortisol is released in response to fear or stress by the adrenal glands as part of the fight-or-flight mechanism." —Psychologytoday

I have learned throughout my life that I can argue with friends and family about a million things, "Mike Trout is a better hitter than Miguel Cabrera" or "Julia Roberts is the best actress ever," but something I will always lose to is science. We can't argue with science. The quote above from Psychologytoday is possibly the most important one you'll read throughout this book because it is irrefutable. The fact of the matter is that if you are a complainer, chances of good health decrease as you get older. For those TV fans out there, you don't have to be Chris Traeger (Rob Lowe) from Parks and Rec who is over the top with his positivity and fitness regimen (borderline to the point of being annoying). But the more positive we are in our daily lives, the more likely we are to live a long and happy life.

"A half hour of complaining every day physically damages a person's brain, according to research from

Stanford University. Whether you're the one griping or you're the one listening, exposure to negativity peels back neurons in the hippocampus – the part of the brain used for problem solving and cognitive function. Over time, complaining becomes a habit. If you're surrounded by complainers, then you're more likely become one." –Stephanie Vozza

There are several adages that people use throughout life such as, "You are what you eat" or "You are who you hang out with"…not sure if that is an actual adage, but it should be. This is 100% the case when talking about the people you spend your time with. Sometimes it's inevitable; you're at a family party and you can't escape the crazy cousin that whines about all that's wrong in his/her life. For the most part, we control who we hang out with. Spending time with friends or family that are constant complainers can have negative repercussions on your brain. While growing up, we have choices of the clicks we'd like to be a part of. For some people, they are more open-minded and don't really have a specific group of people they spend time with. Whoever you choose to be around for a majority of your days, think to yourself, if these people are making you a happier person or leading you down a negativity path. Everyone should want to have positivity surround them in their daily lives.

As we continue to try to better our lives, there are many things we can do or practice that will help us be happier. Simply put, complaining less in your daily life will lead to more positivity and confidence. We will talk more about changes we can make in Chapter 5.

Chapter 3: Types of Complainers

There are several different types of complainers that we encounter throughout our lives. As I go through this next chapter, you are all going to realize you have certain friends and acquaintances that fit into these categories. Perhaps more importantly, you may even realize that you are in one of these categories. While reading, if one pops out that may be you, it is a good thing because now you are aware and have the ability to face the facts and make a change to better your life and be more optimistic.

The three types of complainers, in reverse order of how annoying they can be, are:
- The Attention-Getter
- The Passionate Complainer (also known as the 'Emotional Complainer')
- The Blob Complainer (molds any situation into a complaint)

The third most annoying type of complainer is the 'Attention Getter'. This is a person who voices something negative with the goal of getting people to notice them more than others. In my opinion, the biggest perpetrator of this type of complaining is the news. News stations normalize complaining. The goal of a news company is to have a bigger story that can "one-up" their competitors, which is usually negative. The negative stories seem to get so much more publicity than the positive ones; and to me that's a travesty.

The complaining epidemic on television and social media has trickled from politics to sports in recent years. Just like how we rarely see shows celebrating politicians who selflessly help their communities, or how we focus on the things athletes are *not* rather than what they *can* be. The highest programming seems to be a couple people on TV yelling and arguing about why conservatives or liberals are bigger idiots or why LeBron James will never be as good as Michael Jordan. But what if we spent more time discussing how great LeBron James is and applaud his accomplishments rather than compare him for the sake of putting him down? The constant comparing and judging of our current leaders in politics and sports makes it tough for anyone to watch with enjoyment. Everything can be spun into a negative; but, can everything be spun into a positive?

That brings me to my next point; athletes are great examples of complainers. I have been in sports my entire life and I understand that it is difficult to keep your cool at times. There are endless examples of players complaining about payment structures, verbally dismantling opponents in the media, and even complaining about their coaches or teammates. As an athlete, there is so much to be thankful for. These men and women are being paid for something that most of them love to do. The major sports in particular get paid extremely well for their work. They have the ability to be positive role models for kids around the globe. Maybe some athletes have the secret recipe; the more negativity they can bring into their lives, the more attention they will receive from the media (*sarcasm intended*).

I have yet to watch a professional sporting event in which a player or coach did not argue, 'palms up' to the official, or roll around on the ground in fake agony (which *is* a form of a complaint -- I'm looking at you, soccer). Looking at an official with 'palms up' screams, "Look at me! You blew the call ref!" Players spend way too much time looking for attention by complaining during a sporting event. If a basketball player takes the ball to the hoop and misses the shot, he'll look at the ref with his palms up as if he were fouled. When a wide receiver has tight coverage and doesn't make the catch, he'll look at the ref with his palms up as if it were pass interference. It is an issue in sports and it is not helping the future generation of athletes.

Another group of attention-getters that we all know well are children. And I was the Babe Ruth of complaining as a child. I remember growing up with my awesome family in San Diego, California and I was a *HUGE* complainer. When I didn't get my way, I would threaten to run away. Really, I would just go to a small walkway through a weed infested lot about a block from my family's house. If I wanted something as small as going to my brother's baseball practice but wasn't allowed to go, I would wait in that walkway for about 15 minutes hoping my parents would come chasing me. But this was in the era when kids actually went outside, so my parents knew I would be safe in the neighborhood. Plus, they knew I'd come loping like Eeyore back into the house after my pouting session and go straight into my room. If this were like a game of poker I would have lost a lot of money because my parents called my bluff every time.

Kids complain. We have all seen the kid in the grocery store yelling and crying that their parents won't buy something they want. The parents that don't cave in are more likely to have their kids grow up without the idea that complaining equates to getting things. If we allow complainers to get what they want when they are young, the brain is trained to function as, "When I complain, I get what I want." Obviously, that is not the way we want to train our future leaders.

The next type of complainer is the passionate complainer (or emotional complainer). The passionate complainer is someone that constantly complains about their body issues, relationship problems, or lack of self-worth. Passionate complainers are difficult to talk about because it can make people feel quite uncomfortable. Many of us have this person in our lives that talks to us about all of their personal problems. There is a fine line with this topic; most of us will just wear it and be a sounding board for people that need to be heard. There are ways to get yourself out of these (usually awkward) situations or even better, help these people with their problems so they don't use you as their personal diary.

I understand that some people who voice complaints need genuine medical or therapeutic help. They may battle with mental health issues on a daily basis, and their complaints are the best they know how to ask for help. However, these are not the people I'm talking about. The most popular emotional complaint that I've heard throughout my adult years is usually about someone's body. This isn't the easiest topic to discuss with people because there are many people that get extremely self-conscious. There are even people in great shape that feel this way at times. As a listener to these complainers, you need to be sure not to overstep your boundaries. Usually people with body issues don't need a lot of feedback, they just need someone to listen. They know what is necessary to make a change in their life, they just need to commit to it; whether that change is physically, psychologically, or both.

We are at a time in society where most of what we see on TV, in magazines and other marketing material, is attractive/fit people. Looking like Carrie Underwood or Chris Hemsworth isn't what will make us happy. We need to have an overall goal of what we want to do, and daily goals of how to achieve that. Sometimes, you can even be happy without making a change. Finding confidence inside your own skin is not an easy task, but it is possible.

Another aspect of the passionate complainer is the person that always whines about their relationship problems. This can be someone that struggles to find companionship or people that are in long-term relationships. We are bombarded every day with various ways to meet people on social media and other technology outlets.   Many of us find ourselves in situations where a few relationships or dates haven't gone as planned and the thought of finding a spouse down the road seems unrealistic. Usually, love is difficult to find. It takes lots of trial and error before finding that right fit. If long-term is what you are looking for, complaining about how bad things are in the dating world isn't going to help. Commit to being the best version of yourself and stay positive.

You can complain about how unfair dating is *or* you can continue to find ways to surround yourself with good people and patiently wait for that special someone to come along. Life is filled with single people, you just have to know where to find the good ones (and they're not all in one spot where you can just "swipe right"). Put some confidence into your search and trust your judgement. Your friends and family will hopefully be there along the way to help, but regularly emptying your heart might not be the most constructive way to vent. Exude a positive light and you will attract the right people.

People in relationships can also find ways to include complaining into their daily routine. There is no such thing as a perfect relationship. "You're not perfect, sport. And let me save you the suspense; this girl you met, she isn't perfect either. But, the question is whether or not you're perfect for each other. That's the whole deal. That's what intimacy is all about.

Now you can know everything in the world, sport, but the only way you finding out that one is by giving it a shot." This famous quote by Robin Williams from *Good Will Hunting* says a lot. We all have ideas in our heads about what a healthy relationship looks like, but it is difficult to mirror what we see on TV. Relationship problems will arise, how we handle them is the determining factor. Small issues such as doing the dishes or cleaning the house are bound to come up. Couples need to understand that these daily battles need to be discussed. In many cases, larger issues such as lack of communication or lack of passion occur. Don't find a friend and complain about your personal problems unless that person can supply you with some answers on how to better your situation. Talk to your significant other. Sweeping your issues under the rug and complaining to friends and family just so the problem can come back into your life at some point is not the best way to handle it.

The final type of complainer and by far the worst...the blob complainer. This is the person in your life that molds anything into a problem. They complain about every little thing that doesn't go their way. It is a toxic way to live your life.

Your friend asks you, "How is work going?" Let's imagine work isn't going all that well.

There are two routes to that answer:
1) "I'm exhausted. So busy all the time. My coworkers are lazy. My boss doesn't understand."
2) "I've had some challenges this week, but I'm doing really great work and I've got food to eat!"

Neither expresses sheer joy for a job that might be better left undiscussed, but the second one makes the pain temporary and the benefits long-lasting. Which person sounds more fun to talk to?

I don't want to list all of the things that the blob complainer whines about because the list would never end. But here are a couple examples I thought of off the top of my head.

You and your wife are having a Super Bowl party. There are going to be five families at your house with plenty of food and drink. Instead of enjoying the company, food, and game, you can't stop complaining to your wife about cleaning the house and doing the dishes when everyone leaves. It is a great time with people you care about, but the misery of cleaning overpowers your *present* feelings of joy. We oftentimes worry about the future and miss what's right in front of our faces!

Next, you have a great job with a company you enjoy. Your salary is well above average but you continue to see that you are racking up debt. Instead of learning how to become a more responsible person financially, you complain to your family and friends about your lack of money. It is not a problem of making money or enjoying your job, your mind immediately takes you to the negatives of your spending problems. Why not find ways to save instead of complaining about your spending issues?

This blob complainer has so much negative energy oozing throughout their body, that people don't want to be around them. Everyone and everything in the world is out to get this person. They can't catch a break! Their job sucks, they don't have a significant other, their friends don't have time for them...the list goes on. They need to grab ahold of their life and figure out how to make a change.

We can all get caught in this trap and not even realize it. When you run into this person, every time a negative topic comes up, change it. See how many times you can turn that complaint into something good and positive. This may help that person realize how much of a downer they are. If they don't want to be helped, stay away from this person because they can only bring you down. I'm not telling you to abandon your friends, but there does come a time where we all have to ask if certain connections are making our lives better or not. It's not selfish to give yourself distance if an "energy-sucker" isn't willing to make an effort to get happy!

Now I need to point out, complaining isn't the same as getting things off your chest. There are definitely times when getting your feelings out is a positive thing. If you work a job and your boss often asks you to complete tasks that make you uncomfortable, it is not complaining to set your boundaries. If you are feeling genuinely depressed and want to seek help from a friend or a professional, it's important to reach out and be honest with yourself. However, these aren't the people about whom I am talking. The complainers I call to mind are those whose lives are not improved by calling attention to their little annoyances. They are the ones who say things that would be best left unsaid.

These types of whiners bring to mind a famous episode from the sitcom Seinfeld. In this episode, one of the main characters father, Frank Constanza, invents a holiday called "Festivus." The holiday has a number of odd traditions, but one in particular applies to complaining: "The Airing of Grievances." According to Frank, this is where the family meets around the dinner table, and you "tell them all the ways they have disappointed you over the past year."

Frank: I got a lot of problems with you people, and now you're gonna hear about it!... Kruger, my son tells me your company stinks!... You couldn't smooth a silk sheet if you had a hot date with a babe... (places hands on his head) I've lost my train of thought.

This is a very extreme example, but the fact that Frank isn't even able to keep his thoughts straight through a single complaint shows just how unimportant it is. Like this character, we turn our own brains into mush when we dwell on issues that we are not actively trying to improve.

However, if Frank were to actually talk through these problems and work toward a solution that benefits himself and others, that is not complaining. When we have problems with a person or group of people, it is a good thing to put them on the table and try to resolve them. If we bottle that negative energy up, it can lead to bigger issues.

This also happens in relationships; someone doesn't like the way their boyfriend, girlfriend, husband, wife, or significant other does something and they just let it go. If you don't like the fact that your husband doesn't kiss you goodbye anymore when you leave for work, you should tell him because that small change in your morning routine could uplift the rest of your day.

It is not a complaint; it is a concrete, fixable way to help you both begin your day on a positive note.

Chapter 4: No One Feels Sorry for You

The next couple of chapters are going to be a little tougher for some of you to read. I'm going to be blunt about some truths that I've learned on my journey, and it might sound negative at times. But when life feels like it is not going well for us, sometimes we have to face harsh truths. One of these truths is something I have heard from college baseball coaches for the past decade: "No one feels sorry for you."

Wake up for 6:00am weights, class at 8:00am, class at 10:00am, study hall, practice at 2:00pm, study and homework, bed, wake up and do it all over. It is a difficult schedule to maintain for many student-athletes; however, there are thousands of college kids that wish they were in the same situation as these extremely fortunate athletes and many of them spend too much time complaining about how demanding it is.

In almost everything we do, there are scores of people around the world who would trade places with us in a heartbeat. Your workout is too strenuous? You have working legs! Your gas bill was too high? You have a warm house! I'm not trying to suggest that your problems do not matter, but no one is going to feel sorry that the icing on your cake is a little smudged when you have a nice cake to begin with! IT CAN ALWAYS GET WORSE!

There are different outlooks we can have in life when we get pushed to the ground. Carol Dweck, author of *Mindset*, distinguishes the characteristics of a "fixed mindset" versus a "growth mindset" – something that alters how we view certain situations in our daily lives. She asserts that, "People with a *fixed mindset* – those who believe that abilities are fixed – are less likely to flourish than those with a *growth mindset* – those who believe that abilities can be developed." I want to simplify what she discusses throughout the book. The idea of fixed mindset vs. growth mindset is a concept that we can all use to benefit many situations in our lives.

When our coaching staff at UOP was let go back in 2015, I definitely had the "fixed mindset." I thought I got screwed, there was nothing I could do about it, and I must just not be good enough. At the time, I should have listened to my mom – the master of the growth mindset. She told me it would be a great learning experience, and if I wanted another opportunity, I would know how to take advantage of it next time. With the growth mindset, I would think about why it happened and how I could become better because of it.

I knew I wanted to be a pitching coach at the collegiate level. At UOP, I had only helped with offense, so when I left in 2015 after only one season I was not experienced enough for the various pitching coach vacancies around the nation. Thankfully, by the time I got hired as the volunteer coach at SDSU, Mom's words had set in and I took the opportunity to learn.

I was able to coach under Sam Peraza, one of the most popular and well-respected pitching coaches in the country. I followed him, listened to him, and became close friends with him. Strangely, once I leaned in to the task of learning, I actually had a blast growing as a person, and I even made a life-long friend. After two years, I learned so many ins and outs of his program that I was prepared for the next great opportunity. It makes me laugh to think how unprepared I would have been if the next job had just been handed to me because "I deserved it," whatever that means.

Again, no one felt sorry for me that I was working at a great school, in a great city, for a great program, near my family. There was a period where I dwelled on the negatives and complained daily, but once I realized that there were literally thousands of coaches that wished they were in my shoes, I was grateful and started giving 100% effort in everything I did.

When you are able to do a job, any job, to the best of your ability, you can at the very least be proud of what you worked towards. Usually we continue to look forward to the next job, task, trip, etc. This is why rewarding yourself becomes so important. After you complete something, you need to reward yourself. It makes those jobs worthwhile and gives you something to work for. Celebrating *every* success isn't totally necessary (you don't need a trip to Disneyland for tying your shoes), but when you've been building a patio in your back yard for several weeks and you complete the job, praise your accomplishments. Go out to dinner with a couple friends and have drinks. If we continually move on to the next thing without celebrating our victories, what is the point of success?

My wife and I bought our first house in August 2018. When we made the purchase, a lot of work had to be done to the back yard; it was a dirt lot. As we were designing what we wanted it to look like, things in the new house seemed to start piling up that needed to be addressed. Our furnace wouldn't pass inspection, our water heater broke, the plumbing backed up twice; the list wasn't small.

The fixed mindset version of Joey would have said, "This is annoying, we bought a bad house and there's nothing we can do." Notice how personal, permanent, and helpless that line of thought is. There is no room for a happy ending. The growth mindset Joey said, "Luckily these problems happened to us at our first house. We now know how to fix a lot of issues and what to look for when we are going through the inspection process next time." The problems were new wrinkles in my brain – not bad things that happened to me; they were solvable and temporary; and they were fixable! Spinning negative situations into positive ones takes practice, just like anything. You have to visualize and train your brain to handle adversity. Julie and I were also newlyweds at the time and were able to work on all these small projects together, which was awesome. They weren't always fun projects, but the fact that we were able to get through these minor issues together was a great starting point for our marriage.

We had days that were very frustrating for the both of us. But we had a date in mind that we wanted the back yard to be completed. We battled through some annoying "first world problems," and I'm proud to say that Julie's complaining was minimal throughout this entire process. Most people could have let the negative situation get to them. We stayed with the process and had the yard completed by our estimated date. The weekend of October 12th was our celebration of success. We had family and friends over that weekend and enjoyed spending time in the new house and in the newly designed yard. All of that chaos for weeks was worth it, because our end goal was to have things done in time. We worked towards that goal and were fortunate enough to have a great weekend with people that we care about. In fact, by the time our friends were over laughing with drinks and food, it was almost like the problems were gone with the snap of a finger.

I didn't realize it as a child or young adult, but growing up in San Diego didn't give me a great perspective of what life is actually like. I lived where people vacation -- minutes from the beach and the best weather in the country. There was never a dull moment in San Diego because there is always something *else* to do. I had some extremely wealthy friends and didn't really know what it was like not to be able to do things or have things. My parents were middle class folks, but I felt like I was rich because they were able to give me everything I needed for a wonderful childhood.

Cell phones were just starting to get really popular when I was in middle school. Not many kids had them unless their parents had money. One day at school, one of my good friends dropped his phone and it broke. Initially I thought, "That sucks! His Mom is gonna be pissed." After he started complaining (it was 100% his fault by the way), he began to think of excuses to tell his parents of how it happened and why it wasn't his fault. I remember telling him that he should just tell them the truth. What's the worst that could happen? They don't get you a new phone for a while? He mentioned to me that if it wasn't his fault, maybe his parents would get him a new one without asking questions.

This is where it gets comical; the next words he said to me out of his 12-year old mouth were, "I *NEED* a phone!" It's probably difficult for some people to understand this, but in 1999, it was rare to have a cell phone if you were not in high school or college. All I could think about at that point was how ridiculous he sounded. What 12-year old needs a phone that bad? This poor kid is complaining about losing an object that he spent 5 hours a day playing snake on when there are kids that we are going to school with every day that are living below the poverty line. In his defense, Snake was the best cell phone game of all time, but there are people all over the world that are homeless, hungry, and sick. Have some perspective.

This is an example of a useless complaint, but I do realize that some situations or objects may be more important on a relative level to some than others. For some of us, losing a mere phone is a big deal; for others, losing a job is reality. Whatever adversity hits us, we need to practice getting better at it. If we don't deal with too much adversity throughout the beginning stages of our lives, when we get into a situation that requires us to overcome, we may not be prepared. That could be anything in life. When we grow up getting everything that we want, we don't know how to deal with failure; and in turn, we grasp onto the idea of complaining when things don't go perfectly for us.

There are two types of people when it comes to adversity, those that crumble or hide when it hits them, and those that push themselves to overcome obstacles. The people that crumble end up feeling sorry for themselves and want the attention of others because of their deficiencies or setbacks. In the end, they are setting themselves up for failure.

A lot of people quit when something gets in their way, but sometimes we can find examples of people who force their way into success because of relentless work ethic and positivity. Jim Carrey was homeless at one point in his life; Benjamin Franklin dropped out of school at age 10; Franklin Roosevelt became partially paralyzed at age 39. There are so many great people that can be at the forefront of our adversity talk. Let me start with an example of minimal adversity that I dealt with at a younger age and then I'll tell two stories about people that have had to dominate adversity throughout their lives.

In 4th grade, I had my friend David Garcia give Lindsy Walker a letter asking her to be my girlfriend because that's how I did things back then. She circled yes, and we proceeded to have a long-term 4th grade relationship: one month. After that magnificent month of hanging out on the blacktop together, I had David give Lindsy another letter saying I didn't want to be her boyfriend anymore. I found a way to avoid risk of failure and, thus, adversity.

But two years later, I had a change of heart. I walked up to Lindsy, face to face, on the hill leading to the basketball courts at San Marcos Middle School. I wasn't going to be a coward this time, because I was a confident young man (you know how in 6th grade you know everything already?). Well, when I asked her if she'd be my girlfriend, I did it in front of 15 people or so, and to my shock, she said, "I just want to be friends." Thirty eyes swung to me.

I felt like Sammy Sosa had taken a bat to my stomach when those words came out of her mouth. Now I had to turn around and walk through a line of friends who just saw me get rejected. I had to pretend like it didn't hurt my feelings or ego, and I had to convince them I wasn't a "loser."

That is just a small sample of what it's like to go through some adversity, but it was the first time I had ever been turned down and really embarrassed in front of a group of people. I didn't realize it at the time, but when we get told 'No', it can make us stronger. We have more reasons to work. Feeling sorry for myself and reacting in a negative way would only prolong my 6th grade suffering. And sometimes, "No" can just give us a dose of reality. There was really nothing to complain about – she didn't want to be my girlfriend. This was a learning moment for me, and just one of many stories in my life where I had to overcome adversity.

I tell this story as more of a silly, relatable anecdote than anything else. I know it wasn't true adversity. But there are people out there who have had to face adversity far greater than what 6th grade Joey could have imagined as he slunked away from his first rejection. From an adversity standpoint, there are some great people out there that everyone should learn about.

Shaquem Griffin is an athlete that has stomped on *real* adversity. He somehow made it to the NFL with <u>one arm</u>. Let me repeat: in a sport that requires Olympic level athleticism and coordination, Griffin was playing without a vital body part. How easy would it have been for him to quit?

But he didn't. He had a skilled brother who constantly challenged him to be better, faster, stronger. He found a way to excel in high school and then college. He couldn't catch passes from a quarterback, so he found a way to bat them down. When he couldn't do that, he'd just use his strong physical frame to make strong tackles and dislodge the ball. Instead of focusing on what he *couldn't* do, he found ways to be better at what he could.

I'm sure there were times when he was growing up that he didn't feel he was given a fair chance, but instead of rolling over and moaning about it, he worked his way up to the 46-man roster on the Seattle Seahawks.

My favorite example is a guy that I just recently learned about. I was watching a YouTube show called "Maxout" that is hosted by Ed Mylett. He had a guest on one day named Nick Santonastasso. On paper, Nick seemed like a pretty awesome dude. He was a high school wrestler, turned into a professional body builder and model with over 400k followers on Instagram.

Without knowing anything else, anyone would think he seemed to have it together.

But what makes Nick so interesting that I haven't told you, is that Nick has no legs, one arm, and one finger. When I began watching, all I could think about was how bad I felt for Nick. He was born with a rare disease, had to be in a wheelchair, and couldn't do every day things that we all take for granted.

After watching this hour-long interview, Nick had completely changed the way I thought about him. I didn't feel sorry for him; I wanted to have an attitude as good as his every day. This is a person that could have very easily folded the hand that he was given in life. Instead of feeling sorry for himself, he found ways to get things done by himself. He challenged himself to think outside the box. I would say that Nick has a strong growth mindset. Growing up he didn't tell himself, "I can't tie my shoes," he found ways to get it done.

Nick's parents didn't hand him everything. When he needed something, they told him to find a way to complete the task. They weren't being mean, they were being helpful. If Nick wanted to live a fulfilled life, he would need to learn to get things done on his own. He has turned into one of the most inspirational people I've learned about and is a great role model for anyone that needs some extra motivation.

Next time you want someone to feel bad for a situation you're in, think about Nick and Shaquem and how uplifting and positive they have been to so many people throughout their lives; then take a step back, gather yourself, and find a way to make things better. We get one opportunity at life and adversity comes in all different shapes and sizes. What type of person are you going to be when it inevitably steps into your life?

Chapter 5: Make a Change...Be Happy

The #1 thing that people complain most about in life...their job. For those who are not yet in the working world, their source of complaints – or their "job" – is school. So many people out there believe that their job is who they are. Your job is simply what you do. How can we avoid **becoming** what we do? Once again, it involves listening to something we've all heard: **do something you love**.

People who know me would probably agree that my name and baseball have been synonymous throughout my life. I have played, coached, scouted, organized, or just watched baseball without taking so much as a week off since I was one year old; my life hasn't just been surrounded by this great game – it is this game.

But when I finally quit baseball in 2011, after one year in the Minor Leagues, I didn't really know where I was going to go next. It was like getting a divorce or losing a loved one. Suddenly, waking up in the morning didn't have a next logical step. I didn't need to work out, to throw, to be anywhere. Most people I knew were shifting their life goal toward how to earn money, but I didn't really have a path planned that didn't involve baseball.

So, I improvised the best I could. My first job out of pro ball was at a company called California Cedar Products in Stockton, CA. I helped run the website and blog for pencils.com. This company had a mission to help children in the community. I embraced the culture and it introduced me to kind, hardworking colleagues whom I admired for their dedication. I felt valuable working there, and I was satisfied with the pay. But I was at a desk for 8+ hours a day researching and writing about pencils.   Nothing against the Blackwing, the single-most impressive pencil in the history of lead, but it was difficult for me to get excited about work every day.

I also lived with my girlfriend at the time and the relationship was blossoming. We had been together for over a year and we seemed to be on the same page about where things were headed. We had a plan about our future together and working at California Cedar Products and living with her had us on the right track.

I suppose I could have complained about how boring and unfulfilling my job was, even though I was a 23-year-old with steady work and no problem affording my bills. I could have made sarcastic jokes about how much Mondays stunk or how long Friday felt. Or I could have just found something I liked.

Five months into working for California Cedar Products, an acquaintance of mine called to offer me a position running a baseball training facility he planned to open in San Diego. I had run into a fork in the road. I could stay at Cal Cedar and continue living with my girlfriend, or take a job nearly 500 miles away. Despite all of the "safe" reasons I could have stayed in Stockton, I knew what I had to do.

I ran the Brickyard Cages in San Diego for two years. The money in helping kids with their swings was a little better than pencil-pushing, but I was still making less than most of my buddies. I was able to learn what it was like to run a business and I met some great people along the way. There were a number of current and former MLB players that would come in to get their off-season swings at the Brickyard. I listened, asked questions, watched how they worked, and it helped me develop a better understanding of how things are done at the highest level.

The first year at the Brickyard was great. I was able to help kids, work with some great people, and I was in the baseball industry. I also re-structured my salary so I was able to take more of the money from our youth camps. The more kids that I was able to get to our camps, the bigger paycheck I would get. I started saving a good amount of money and I began feeling like things were even better than before.

As time went on, the job became more stressful. The owners were not making the financial returns they were hoping for. I was working 10-12 hour days 6-7 days a week. I was only 25-years-old at the time and just starting to realize what the working world was like. The owners told me to have our hourly employees work less so the owners did not have to pay them as much. I completely understood from their standpoint; they wanted to make more money. This was bad news for me and the other workers. They wanted more hours and I couldn't give them what they were asking for. I was a salaried employee making more money than any of the owners. I was getting worn down with the amount of time I was spending running the facility.

After two years at the Brickyard, I was in another difficult position. The employees and I battled with each other daily about how unfair the hours and pay structures were. They complained to me and I complained to the owners (I also complained to any of my friends and family that would listen). Should I stay at the Brickyard? A place where the working environment was leading me to an unhappy daily life? At this point, I was making good money and had nothing else on the horizon. How could I leave?

Towards the end of my tenure at the Brickyard, I met with a self-made man named Nils Forssman one day and he gave me some great advice. He had come to the U.S. after living in South Africa and started a company in San Diego that was very successful. "Go after success, not money," he told me.

I found myself complaining more and more towards the end of my Brickyard days. No matter what I did, there was someone that would be upset with me. I couldn't make the owners and the employees happy...it was one or the other. After weeks and months of trying to find anything that would make me happy again, something happened. Finally, there was a sign that I needed a change. It was a Monday afternoon, one of the owners had come in to talk to me about the payment structure again. He told me that the owners had decided to minimize the hours of all hourly employees again (they had already done this once), as well as limit the amount of workers that I could hire for youth camps. This meant more work for me and the Assistant Manager, Brandon. I needed that extra nudge to make a change. After two years, I decided to quit the Brickyard with no other full-time position waiting for me.

I then made the decision to start my coaching career. In only three years, I had gone from a job with just enough money, to a job with a comfortable salary and benefits, to a job where I'd be scraping by – but I found myself complaining less often. I coached baseball at Francis Parker High School, substitute taught at Cathedral Catholic High School, and scouted part-time for the Baltimore Orioles. I loved the idea of telling people, "I scout for the Orioles." That definitely was an enjoyable job at times, but coaching was the best work experience I had. I loved the relationships that I was building with these high school kids. I felt that they truly respected me and I had an impact on so many of their lives.

After my one year at Francis Parker High School, I was offered the head coaching job at The Bishop's School. This was a small private school that needed some help building a winning culture. They also needed some upgrades to their facilities. I went into the situation with hopes of turning the program around. I spent the first couple of months connecting with parents and working on fundraising. I had some great relationships and it seemed as though I would be able to make some significant changes for the better. This was my first head coaching job at the high school varsity level. I was new and did not know how to handle all of the attention from parents.

We raised a good amount of money in the first few months and were ready to start upgrading our "sandlot" of a ballpark. Just as we were ready to begin on field renovations, we hit a road block. The athletic director felt that I was trying to do too much, too fast. He recommended that I make some minor cosmetic changes before jumping into anything too big. This was a problem for me and the program. I complained to parents that I wasn't getting enough help from the athletic department. I had no knowledge of this at the time, but some parents teamed up and went in to discuss plans with our AD. He was quite upset that I had lost control of the parents in my program and they were beginning to cause problems. I had created a complaining monster and didn't even realize it! Before I knew it, me along with all of the team parents were whining about what we *didn't have.*

I spent the season battling with athletic administration and the parents. It was not a great situation and once again, I found myself complaining about how unfair things were.

It took a few jobs for me to realize what I really loved. For a short period of time, I knew the feeling of going to bed at night, and dreading going to work in the morning. But I can say with all honesty that when I go to bed on Sunday nights now, I am excited for Monday morning. This is a shift that many people can make in their lives if they devote themselves to making difficult changes that may seem daunting in the moment. Most people who dislike their work lives fear that making a change would not only make little improvement, but it could make their lives harder in the process. But there is always risk in self-improvement; those dedicated to living their truest, happiest lives find a way to make it work. I consider myself a good example, having gone a few of my earning years as a volunteer. It was hard, but now I look forward to Monday – not Friday.

This sentiment is something that Gary Vaynerchuk addressed in a podcast called *The Garyvee Audio* Experience. In the interview, he said he feels bad for people that look forward to Friday. He states, "I'm blown away by people celebrating the end of the week. Like the weekend is your escape from your reality." I completely agree! What are you doing with your lives from Monday-Thursday that makes you so miserable? If that's the way you feel, you are wasting away over half of your life. Stop complaining about your unfulfilling job and do everything in your power to get into a field that you are more passionate about.

I understand that for a mid-20's single person, it is easier to make changes than a 40-year-old with three children. However, I do feel that if you are truly unhappy with what you are doing with your life, you *must* make a change. The average person sleeps 8 hours, is awake 16 hours, and works *HALF* of those 16 hours (not including weekends). This would mean you are miserable for nearly half of your life that you're awake. If you devote yourself to finding something that you are passionate about, even if you don't make as much money, you will feel more fulfilled in your daily life.

Another way to make a positive change in your life... When I wake up in the morning, I think of one thing that can help me start my day on a positive note. My default has become my wife, Julie. I try to shake it up and find gratitude in various ways, but often my brain goes directly to her, which is natural because I'm most grateful for her. But it doesn't have to be a person. It can literally be anything you are happy about in your life – job, parents, even something as small as the first breath you take in the morning. Not everyone got to take that first breath today! Then, after your day is complete and you are about to go to bed, do the same thing. Be thankful you have a bed, some blankets, and a pillow or two.

This is the same concept that we hear about in relationships. You don't ever want to start or end your day in an argument with your significant other. It is better to forget about whatever problem may be causing stress for the two of you and finish the day with an "I love you."

Find a simple hobby. There are endless hobbies that people have throughout their lives that bring them happiness. Lots of complainers sit around and don't do much with their free time. Instead of wasting away your life, find something that you can do that you have fun with. We have the internet. Even for those people that don't like to go out and experience nature or sports, a hobby for you can be to get online and compete in the gaming world. Maybe you like the idea of getting online and doing graphic design for enjoyment. It's always a good idea to mix in some physical activity, but you don't have to be a cross country runner to stay in decent shape.

You can also find things to do with friends and family. Men: set aside a poker night with your buddies once a month. Ladies: go to a happy hour with your girlfriends once a month. Sometimes the men and ladies can switch. Whatever makes you smile. Surround yourself with upbeat friends that you can enjoy spending some free time with. Those outings can drastically change your outlook and help your positivity meter climb the ladder. It is also a great idea to be around people more often than not. Alone time is necessary, but locking yourself in a room alone for hours can get depressing.

I have an example or what I'm talking about and he is very close to me, my Dad. When he sits at home and watches the news, he is the champion of complaining. I don't even want to bring up politics when we're in the same room anymore, because everything is a problem. Then you have the other side of Big Lou; the retired guy that enjoys going to Scrabble night once a week. He will talk your ears off about the 70-point word he used to beat last week's champion. When he finally gets off his favorite recliner, he goes on walks for anywhere from 30 minutes to a couple of hours. He learns things. The past couple of years he has enjoyed learning the language of his ancestors, Italian, with an online app, and he looks forward to future travel to Italy where he can communicate verbally with them. The one constant in my father's hobbies? Action. He gets up and does something.

There are so many hobbies out there that can increase our happiness and, at times, self-worth. We all have the ability to find things that we enjoy; the problem that many of us have is finding the time to fit these into our daily lives. There is an easy answer that is one of the best slogans of all time by Nike: just do it.

We need to continue to find ways to enjoy ourselves for our own sanity. Get out of the house, get away from your kids, get away from your job, and go do something with a friend or group of friends that will fill that void. Routines are great, but when the routine gets tedious and boring, negativity will start to set it. Beat it to the punch and throw a curveball in your daily routine so your body understands that your brain is in charge.

One of the greatest benefits of making all of these changes is that it can lead to greater optimism, a trait that has a strong correlation to success.

A psychologist who devoted much of his life's research to optimism and pessimism, Martin Seligman, once wrote that "The defining characteristic of pessimists is that they tend to believe that bad events will last a long time, will undermine everything they do, and are their own fault. The optimists, who are confronted with the same hard knocks of this world, think about misfortune in the opposite way. They tend to believe that defeat is just a temporary setback or a challenge, that its causes are just confined to this one case."

This is simple in the case of complainers. Those that have a setback feel that the world is out to get them and there's nothing they can do to change that. Flip that idea around and use those speed bumps in life as learning experiences. Continuing to zero in on the negatives in your life is only going to suck the happiness and energy out of you. Seligman discusses how positive emotions are paired with happy circumstances. Focus on your strengths and the good things in your life and you're more likely to be happy. The happier you are the less you'll complain.

The past is the past. We can all reflect on the good and the bad to help in regards to self-growth, but we also need to be optimistic for our future. The idea that we have things to look forward to in life and goals that we've set out to achieve will make our present life more pleasant. I know it is difficult to enjoy the present if you don't like the situation you're in; but if you understand that your present moment is temporary and you have your eyes set on something bigger down the road, you will be happier now in hopes of accomplishing that goal for the future.

Seligman also discusses a topic that he calls *The Three Dimensions of Happiness*.

The pleasant life: a life that successfully pursues the positive emotions about the present, past, and future

The good life: using your signature strengths to obtain abundant gratification in the main realms of your life

The meaningful life: using your signature strengths and virtues in the service of something much larger than you are

These dimensions of happiness all have positive meanings. "The Pleasant Life" is one that is fairly basic. When someone can successfully obtain positive emotions about their past, present, and future, it can be assumed that they are living a happy life. We all have ups and downs throughout our lives, but the idea that we can systematically focus on all of the good that's happened throughout our past and present, and not dwell on the bad is difficult to achieve. Positive emotions drive us to be positive people.

The second dimension Seligman discusses is "The Good Life." Obtaining abundant gratification in the main realms of your life can mean various things. Some of us put our heart and soul into our family. Some people don't have that ability, and put their energy into their job or a hobby. When you feel fulfilled in the most important areas of your life, you are going to be happy.

I currently don't have my family near me. It is just me and my wife, Julie. When we used to live in San Diego, we were within miles of my entire family. I received more family gratification because I was able to spend time with them on a weekly basis. Now that we have moved up to Northern California, my gratification comes more from work.

"The Meaningful Life" is the final dimension discussed by Seligman. The key word in this dimension of happiness is *service*. When we can use our strengths to benefit something larger than us we will feel whole. For the selfless community, helping others that are less fortunate, or volunteering at a homeless shelter are the types of activities that can truly fulfill your life. That feeling that you get in your gut when you know you've made someone else's day better is indescribable; especially when you know that they haven't had the same opportunities throughout their lives as you have. Spend some of your time in the service of others and you can truly live a meaningful life.

The third aspect of Seligman's dimensions of happiness is crucial for all humans. It leads me into another topic about happiness. There is a documentary titled, "Happy" that I recommend to everyone that could use a positivity boost. Whether you are currently down in the dumps or on top of the world, this film can open your eyes into the beauty of life. The filmmaker, Roko Belic, traveled to several countries searching for the meaning of happiness. There are three stories that were shown throughout the film that caught my heart.

First, he tells the story of Manoj Singh and his family, who live in the slums of Kolkata, India. The space that they all share doesn't look to be more than 75 square feet. He wakes up in the morning and travels to the city where he has the opportunity to drive a rickshaw for a living. This is not a glamorous job by any means, but he is grateful to have something that enables him to make some money to help his family. In the film, he discusses how difficult it is at certain times of the year due to the weather. In the Summer, his feet and head burn, but he keeps on going. He also gets abused by some of the passengers, especially when they are drunk. This man spends his days literally pulling people on a 2-wheeled contraption taking them wherever they need to go, yet after taking a survey for the film, it was shown that he is as happy as the average American.

When Manoj begins talking about his son, you can see his face light up. Every day he comes home from work and his son is waiting for him at a local tea shop. It is refreshing to see someone that – even though by most of our standards in the U.S., he doesn't have much – in the grand scheme of things, he is more grateful and happier than most people simply because he has a job and a family that he loves.

The next story in the film is about a woman named Melissa Moody. She lived on a ranch in Texas with her husband and children. Melissa had a great life until she was run over by a truck after a small altercation with a family member. The truck ran over her head and caused several years of pain, surgeries, and reflection. When something like this happens, no matter what the extent of the injury, it is inevitable for negative thoughts to infiltrate your mind. This was no different for Melissa who, despite going out and trying to live her life as if nothing happened, fell victim to thoughts of depression and suicide. Four years after the accident, her husband divorced her. She also needed more and more surgeries, but she didn't have a job to pay for it. It would have been very easy for Melissa to call it quits.

Instead of giving up, she found work at the San Francisco School for Self-Healing, and after 30 facial reconstructive surgeries and 19 years, she said she's happier than she's ever been. Watching her smile in the film is worth the price of admission. Trying to put yourself in her situation and thinking about how much she has overcome is such an inspiration. Not to mention she chose to spend the rest of her life in the service of others at the Self-Healing center which is a great way to live your life.

Speaking of service to others, another example from the film relates to the famous Catholic nun, Mother Teresa, who opened her first home for dying and destitute people in Kolkata, India. At the time of the film, Andy Wimmer had been volunteering there for 17 years. Prior to that, he was a banking computer manager. He made more money and had more material things, but there was something missing in his life. He feels that helping these people that are struggling with health and have nowhere else to go can give someone a great sense of purpose in life. According to him, "You learn a lot from these patients we care for; for example, acceptance and tolerance." He wants to show these people that someone cares for them, and that his belief is that God is the one who does most. No matter the lesson, he has found more fulfillment in service than in banking.

Now step back and think about what your daily life looks like. Andy Wimmer had a high paying job that he enjoyed, but felt that serving others that are sick and dying was more important than anything else he was going to do. He has devoted his life to serving others that are less fortunate and his happiness meter is through the roof! I can't begin to describe the amount of courage and faith it takes to do what Andy did.

The people described above could have easily been stories turned 180 degrees into lifestyles of negativity and complaining. Manoj has taken the path of gratefulness instead of a complaint-filled life. After extremely difficult times, Melissa decided to devote her life to the service of others when she could have followed the path to darkness. Andy, who seemingly had his life on track, decided that serving others was more fulfilling than his time as a rich person in the banking world.

The decisions may not have been easy ones, but commitment and positivity have led Manoj, Melissa, and Andy to happy lives. Taking the appropriate steps to minimize or stop your complaining takes strong devotion from any individual. There are a few things that may help you when you feel the urge to complain.

Laugh

Laughter increases endorphins and sends mood-lifting dopamine to the brain. This hormone also has the ability to decrease stress levels by helping us experience pleasure. As I have stated before and I will state again, **happiness will lead to less complaining**. If we can find things in our lives that make us laugh, we are more likely to defeat the complaining lifestyle that we have grown accustomed to. It can be as easy as sitting down and watching a funny video.

It is very difficult starting out, but if you can try the exercise below it may help you adjust your mindset.

Whenever I get hurt, burn my finger, smack my knee on the corner of the table, I just start laughing. I have tried to take this into other aspects of my life as well. When I am coaching and an umpire makes a bad call, I laugh. When something unexpected happens in my house and I have to pay more money than I'd like to get it fixed, I laugh. These are minor things that may pop up in your life that you can try to laugh off instead of defaulting to the negative and complain about them. You'll find that a fake laugh at first can lead to an actual one in the end.

Take the course of gratefulness

If you are in a hurry to get somewhere and there is an accident causing traffic, instead of complaining about it, sit in your car and think about something that you're grateful for. Think about where you're coming from or where you are going and how you are grateful for those people or places. Think about how grateful you are to have a car to drive. Think about how grateful you are to listen to music that you enjoy. Also remember that the traffic did not "happen to you" – you are part of it. You *are* traffic. Go back to step one and laugh about that. Any of these thoughts can lift your spirits into a positive mood instead of taking you down the complaining trail.

It is much easier for so many of us to sit in our car and complain. Challenging yourself to consciously understand when those negative thoughts enter your mind is tough. Stop them in their tracks and be grateful. Dr. Scott Jensen, the chair of the Psychology Department at University of the Pacific advises, "Don't just respond, think about the response. Practice the way you respond." If you don't practice how you respond to difficult situations, you can't expect your behaviors to change when those situations arise.

Surround yourself with people that express the behaviors you would like to express

I read an article by Andrew Thomas titled, *7 Scientific Ways to Stop Complaining and Enjoy a Happier Life.* In it, he discusses how you should surround yourself with the right people.

"When trying to stop a bad habit, it helps to surround yourself with people –inspirational speakers or leaders, mentors, family and friends – who embody the same behaviors and discipline you want to live by." An example of this is if you are a smoker and you'd like to quit; you wouldn't surround yourself with people that smoke three packs a day. You would try to be around people that don't smoke at all to help you break the habit.

Look into your relationships: What friends, family, co-workers, or anyone else you spend time with are good people for you to be around? I am not saying that a negative person is a bad person in every case; I am saying that if you want to make a change and attempt to limit the negativity in your life, you should not spend as much time around complainers. This goes for everything in life. When you surround yourself with good, positive people, you are more likely to adapt to those traits and be a positive and happy person.

Serve others

As depicted earlier, serving others is the best way to feel happiness and self-worth. I walked into my office one day and had a sticky note on my door with this written on it:

"The best way to find yourself is to lose yourself in the service of others." –Mahatma Gandhi

I have not taken that sticky note off of my door yet. Spending time with people that may be less fortunate than us opens up our hearts. Serving others comes in many forms. Teaching, coaching, philanthropy, volunteering...there are so many options. Plenty of people get gratification in donating hard dollars to a cause or charity. We all don't have the funds to donate money, but we can always donate time. Building interpersonal relationships is much more powerful than money. Go to a retirement home and spend time with the elderly. Get up and go to an elementary school and spend some time with students by reading to them or tutoring them. Be a big brother or sister. There are endless opportunities in this great world to help others. You don't have to be famous or have a lot of money to be a positive influence on other people.

Write

Writing is a different way to work on limiting your complaining. Writing positive affirmations and systematically putting them in places that you regularly look in your home, car, or office can help build that positivity that you're looking for. I am a huge quote guy. I love reading quotes and putting them in a document that I save, or typing them out on practice plans for my baseball players to read. Reading good quotes and spreading that positive energy around can only help others that may need a little uplifting. Some people like to journal as well and get that pen to paper feeling. Express those grateful feelings in the morning and/or at night in your journal. Even if you had a rough day, write down how you overcame those situations or feelings with positivity. Or maybe that tough day had a couple of situations that you can learn from and handle better in the future. Express that positive loving vibe in your journal and verbally to others. Let your family know that you love them. Tell your co-workers that you appreciate the work that they do. Spread positive vibes to people in your life and you will see that those positive vibes will come back to you.

Chapter 6: Family & Friends

In my life, I have been blessed with friends and family that support me. I want to talk about some people in my life because they have helped me become the person that I am.

I'll start with my brother and sister. My sister, Maria, is an unbelievable human. When I describe her to people it is difficult because she is, in simple terms, the coolest person I know. We are 4 years apart and weren't extremely close socially when we were younger because of the age difference. Maria was one of the 4.0 students in the family that also had success in athletics. Her first two years of college were spent playing softball where she was on a full scholarship. She had an endless group of friends, and from the outside looking in it seemed like she had surrounded herself with high quality people.

Maria was older than me and we didn't spend too much time together other than at the house. I was able to watch her compete in sports for several years of my youth. I always had crushes on her softball teammates and wanted to go to her all-star tournaments. It was enjoyable to watch her blow opponents away with her fastball as I sat in the stands eating as many red vines as my body would allow. People always tended to gravitate towards Maria because of her positive energy. There weren't too many situations while we were growing up that I can remember where she wasn't smiling, singing, or dancing. Her athleticism carried her to a college scholarship, but that was the least of her great qualities.

As we got older, Maria fell into a difficult situation. Seemingly out of nowhere, our parents told us Maria had been kicked out of her college, St. Peter's University in New Jersey.

What could the best person I know have done that could get herself into trouble like that? As it turns out, Maria was expelled because she allegedly neglected her role as the chaperone to a visiting softball recruit. According to Maria and even the recruit herself, they had spent a fun evening at a college party and everything was going fine. When Maria wanted to call it a night, the recruit wasn't quite ready. My sister asked a few of her teammates if they could show the visiting student-athlete around and get her home safely, and they agreed. They did not follow through. The girl that my sister was in charge of was hurt that night and since Maria was the one placed in charge, she was also the one who suffered the consequences: she was kicked out of school.

For the many weeks the school investigated my sister, she would cry on the phone nightly to my parents. At this time, not everyone had cell phones, which meant she had to sit in a public hallway on a payphone, sobbing from 3,000 miles away. When my mom would hang up, she would take the torch and cry some more, knowing that nothing she did could take away the strain of my sister's circumstances. When the school finally concluded that Maria was at fault, it was almost a relief. However, she came home filled with shame and regret.

But almost as quickly as the horrific events of that night unfolded, Maria bounced back. Instead of dwelling on the negative and complaining about her unfair situation, Maria proceeded to leave the school gracefully and apply to Loyola Chicago. She knew that deep down, Loyola was going to be a better opportunity for her. She could have reacted to that situation at St. Peter's and let it negatively affect her for months or even years; but instead, her positivity took over and she wound up in a better place because of it. To this day, I haven't heard my sister mention St. Peter's.

Loyola Chicago turned into a situation that my sister could be proud of. She had stopped playing softball when she left St. Peter's and focused on her academics and social life. She was much happier in Chicago and began to see what her life without sports was going to be like. After a couple years of school, Maria graduated from Loyola Chicago and decided to stay in the city she had grown to love. She lived in downtown Chicago and worked there into her mid-20's. Maria made life-long friends that she continues to stay in touch with while at Loyola. An unfortunate situation at St. Peter's had turned into the best thing that could have happened to Maria.

Many of us are put into uncomfortable situations at various points in our lives. The reaction that Maria had when these difficult times confronted her is how I wish I could have handled any adversity in my life. The best thing about Maria's experience at St. Peter's was that she was kicked out. This can be viewed as a positive or negative experience. Obviously, Maria views this as something that helped mold her into the person she is today. She is a great role model for me and someone that I use in my life as a ray of positivity when something dark arises.

If one high-achieving, older sibling wasn't enough, Louie was a great brother to follow around while I was growing up, too. Unlike my relationship with Maria, Louie and I were together all the time playing video games, whiffle ball, and arguing. There wasn't much that Louie couldn't do. He was the smartest of the 3 siblings, girls found him attractive, and he was athletic, popular, and funny. However, he had one trait that wasn't so admirable: a terrible attitude in failure. When he would foul out of a basketball game in our youth league, he would rip his jersey off like Dennis Rodman and throw it at the bench. When he would strike out in baseball, his eyes would water in rage and his teammates would hide from his inevitable helmet throw. Even as a kid, I knew this was bad... but he was my older brother and I wanted to be like him. So I picked up the bad habit.

I spent lots of time complaining and whining about how Louie would beat me in this or he was better than me at that. Sometimes I would rant and rave just like Louie. I don't think either of us were close to solving our anger issues at all when, one day, twelve-year-old Louie came home wearing a neon pink cast on his arm. Apparently, after a bad at-bat, he punched a dugout wall in anger and shattered his right hand. It was shocking to see how his bad habit led to this, and I was worried that I would do something stupid if I didn't make a change.

Thankfully, Louie learned his lesson, too. When his hand healed, he was calmer. He was no less competitive, but he started finding ways to *win* instead of ways to get mad about losing. Losses against his peers became opportunities for him to learn -- and to beat me in our one-on-one contests.

At that time, he could still throw harder, run faster, and hit with more power than me. I was unaware of it at the time, but just trying to keep up with him was making me a better person in many aspects of my life. We would spend hours in the front yard firing plastic curveballs at each other, shooting rubber hockey pucks into trash cans, or throwing bombs with a football – and he almost always found ways to beat me. To this day, I still jokingly hate the former Major League Baseball player Jermaine Dye, because my brother would imitate his batting stance and hit home run after home run off of me. I just couldn't get him out.

I remember times where my dad would tell me how Louie is older and stronger and I shouldn't worry about the results of our heated front yard battles. As we continued to grow up, I would find myself complaining less and competing more. The complaining that I was doing wasn't going to make anyone feel bad for me, especially my brother. He was going to continue beating me whenever he had the chance. I was lucky to be in this situation because his domination over me had turned me into the ultimate competitor.

As we got older, I started catching up to him in the ability and strength departments. I have never even come close to being on the same level in the smarts department, but we can't have it all. (In fact, he edited much of this book. And I should point out that he didn't revise any sentence that complimented him.) In particular, I began to realize how good I was at baseball. I found myself competing to be better than an older brother for so long, that I had finally found myself in the position of power. Suddenly, the curveballs he used to hit onto our neighbor's roof across the street were diving under his flailing, yellow, plastic bat.

I have always been a confident person, but now I was seeing the development of my body take me to new levels. Confidence is a hard thing to teach. I was in a great situation growing up because I had two older siblings that were great influences on my life. There were so many times that I had to get back up and work harder to be better than Louie. By the time we got to high school, I had an opportunity to show everyone what the last 14 years of losing to him had done to me. I had a chip on my shoulder and I played sports that way for the remainder of my life. I was never the biggest, strongest, or most talented, but you were not going to be able to out-compete me. I truly believe that my lack of complaining as I continued to grow, and my development of competitiveness throughout my life, put me in the position to have success in athletics.

We had competed in the front yard for years against each other. In 2003, we finally had the opportunity to play *with* each other. The competitive battles would continue, but now we were competing against others. The influence that my brother had on me from a competitive standpoint had continued to flourish. We went out that year and had one of the most enjoyable years of my life. There were definitely ups and downs for the both of us, but we kept the complaining to a minimum and pushed each other daily to be the best versions of ourselves.

After winning the section championship that season, I realized that working together *with* my brother had made me even stronger than before. His relentless competitiveness and work ethic molded me into the athlete that I was. Growing does not just stop when you get better, but when you realize you are better together.

My success in athletics throughout my high school years seemed to transfer my confidence into other areas of my life. I was never a great student, but I became a more confident writer which was my strongest attribute in the classroom. I became more confident socially with my friends. I found that from a very young age, my brain had hard-wired itself to set that competitive edge as my default.

Another person that inhibited me from complaining for much of my life was my Dad, Lou. He didn't put up with my shit. Mostly when I would emulate my brother in athletics and throw my helmet or complain when I would strike out or lose a game.

Any sort of defeat made me feel like a failure. Big Lou wouldn't pay any more attention to me than the other players on the team (he was my baseball coach for many years of my youth). In a sense, he was harder on me than any of the other players because his expectations for me were high.

There was one time in particular that I will never forget. I was 11 years old and my travel baseball team was playing a league game at Hawk Heaven, a baseball field my dad built when I was about 10 years old. *Side note, my dad built those two baseball fields without any money. He didn't complain about problems that arose, he just found a way to get donations and free workers and got the job done.* Back to the story, in the 2nd or 3rd inning, I had struck out looking and went back to the dugout in a fit of rage. After throwing my helmet, I was kicked out of the game. It wasn't the umpire that threw me out of the game, but my dad. He sent me to the car where I rolled the windows down and watched my teammates play the next four innings without me. Not only was it embarrassing, but it was an eye-opening moment as well. I realized that complaining about the umpire was going to get me nowhere. I don't ever remember another time in any sporting event where I threw something or cried. I had to re-train my brain how to handle those situations from a young age.

Perhaps the greatest example, though, that I have of a person who is grateful and positive at all times is Clara, my Nonna. She is a true example of someone that is living the American dream. I actually feel bad that I am only going to write about her for this duration...she should have an entire book written about her. As a young girl growing up in Italy during very difficult times, she didn't have much. During WWII, there were several Europeans coming to the East Coast of the U.S. on boats. She had to leave Italy in search for a better life.

She arrived to the U.S. with less than five dollars in her pockets and no plans. Clara ended up traveling to Chicago where she got a job with Mars Candy. My Nonna worked for years, found a husband, and started to build a foundation in the United States. I can't say for certain, but knowing her for the past 30+ years I can say with strong confidence that her complaining throughout these difficult years was minimal-to-non-existent. She knew what she had to do in order to make her life better and she went out and did it. She and her husband, my Nonno, worked full-time jobs – he from sunrise to sundown, she from after dinner until sunrise. They did not complain. Instead, they raised three successful, intelligent children.

I could tell a million Nonna stories, but I am only going to tell one that sticks out to me. I was 8 years old in the Summer of 1995 when my brother and I were in the back yard playing basketball. About two minutes into our warm-ups for the Bulls vs. Magic showdown (we always pretended to be NBA players battling against each other and it was hard to pass up the opportunity to be Michael Jordan and Shaq), we noticed a massive hornet's nest on the eaves of the roof of our house. I had a great attack plan for my brother and me: We would go inside the house, sit down, complain, and do nothing about the bees.

But Nonna was watching us that day. In her sweetest voice, with a thick Italian accent, she asked, "Why you no play outside no more?" We stated our case and were hoping that she would feel bad for us and make us PB & J's with the crust cut off. Instead of joining the complaining party that Louie and I were having, Nonna grabbed a hockey stick from the garage, went outside and beat the shit out of the hornet's nest. She was convincing too because she didn't get stung and the hundreds of bees that seemed to have occupied the hive flew away and out of our lives forever. At that moment, I thought Nonna was a superhero. To this day, I still have never heard Nonna complain about a thing and she is 93 years old. She isn't wired to complain; she is wired to find answers and get things done.

Close-minded Louie and I saw the beehive and said, there's nothing we can do about it. I guess we just can't play basketball today. Open-minded Nonna saw 2 options: 1) Drive Louie and Joey to a park where they can play basketball or 2) Crush the beehive with a hockey stick. Since Nonna had never gotten her driver's license, she went with option 2. I do not want to encourage recklessness with this story. This was simply a situation that entailed a determined grandmother. She wanted Louie and I to enjoy our day and be able to go outside; so, she completed what she felt was the quickest solution.

Who you spend your time with as a kid can tell a lot about what a person is going to be like as they get older. I think the high school years are the most integral years for friend development. My friends and I didn't spend our time together complaining to each other about tests, girls, or any other high school drama. We lifted each other up emotionally, physically, and challenged each other to be the best versions of ourselves.

Surrounding myself with positive people from good families seemed to be an innate skill that I had. I remember my dad getting up to speak at my rehearsal dinner before my wedding. The topic of his talk was how good of friends I had. I never really thought about it because my friends were just my friends and that was the end of it. I didn't compare them to anyone else that could have been my friends. Of all of my close friends, I would undoubtedly say that they've all become successful in their fields of work and family lives. This has benefits that most of us don't even consider. We all communicate on a regular basis and make sure we're all doing well. It is great to have strong positive influences in my life because we support one another even when things aren't all peachy.

Two of my closest friends, Vince Giacalone along with his wife Kendra, are what I would define as heroes. They have 3 awesome kids, however, one of them was born with a rare disease called GM3 Synthase Deficiency. Without going into too much detail, Vince and Kendra didn't know what Gavin would be diagnosed with until a couple years into his life. GM3 Synthase Deficiency causes a lack of brain development and Gavin is extremely susceptible to seizures. Vince and Kendra have had to spend all of their days tending to Gavin's needs. It is a full-time job to make sure he gets the nutrition and care necessary to maintain his health. Gavin is a lucky kid because Kendra and Vince have handled this difficult situation with an unbelievable amount of grace. I know they could spend a majority of their time smiting the lord and complaining about their problems; instead, they take things in stride and work hard together to make the best of the situation.

After about a year of Gavin being diagnosed, they found out he needed a liver transplant so they packed up their bags and moved from San Diego to Pittsburgh to be with a specialist for a few months. They didn't whine about it, they just did it. Vince and Kendra have been such an inspiration to me because I don't know if I would be able to handle a similar situation with as much love and passion as they did. Feeling sorry for themselves would not fix the issue.

I have talked to Vince about Gavin on countless occasions. When I asked Vince how he is so positive about the process, this is how he describes it. "It's the only way we know how to do it." He grew up in a middle-class Italian family with a sister, parents, grandparents, aunts, and uncles that poured love into his life. Complaining wasn't going to heal Gavin. Vince and Kendra knew what they had to do, and put their faith in the process and God.

We all have people in our lives that we can *choose* to look up to. Many of us go with famous or rich people; but I have chosen some people that I am close to. Vince probably doesn't even realize how much of an inspiration he is to me because we had been through a lot together well before Gavin was born. Everyone on the outside looking in (myself included) sees this as a difficult situation for their family. This isn't a difficult situation in their eyes; these are just the lives that God has given them. They go about their daily business of taking care of Gavin and the rest of the family by whatever means necessary. If they need to uproot and go to Pittsburgh, they will do it without a complaint because that is what's best for the family. I admire them more than they'll know and I am proud to call them friends.

Chapter 7: College Years

Moving on from high school to college was tough for me. I moved away from my family and my friends to go play baseball at the University of the Pacific and I was as immature as it gets. I was tied down to a girl in San Diego in what 18-year old me thought was a great relationship. We had only been dating for about a year when I left for college. I felt as though she was the most important person in my life. I did not want to go out to parties with my teammates because I preferred staying alone in my dorm room talking on the phone. It was as pathetic as it sounds. There was one point when I went home 6 weekends in a row! UOP is in Stockton, CA, and that is about 460 miles away from San Diego. It wasn't like I could just hop on my bike and be home in a few minutes. It was an 8-hour drive. I was wasting a great opportunity because I missed my girlfriend and my family? I would complain to my college friends about how bored I was at school and how San Diego was a better place to be. The truth was, I did not experience any of the fun social activities that were happening at UOP. I went to weights, class, did school work, talked on the phone, went to bed, then did it all over again the next day. That is a terrible way to live life...I am telling you from experience. There were only a couple things that kept me somewhat happy during my freshman year. Checking in with my high school friends like Vince to see how life was in the Midwest (he went to school at Bowling Green) was always a good conversation. I was also having some success on the baseball field.

It was no secret to my coaches or my teammates that I was not having a great experience my first semester at UOP. Other than my roommate Joe Oliveira (who regularly called me out for being a complaining little baby), the one person that really knew how miserable things were for me was my Mom.

She never even gave me the option of coming home after the first semester at UOP. The conversations were more along the lines of, "You have a great opportunity. Stop complaining and get the most out of your experience. Most kids wish they could be in your shoes!" The famous saying, "Mom knows best," definitely holds true in this case. I remember going home for Christmas, having a great time with family and friends, then going back up to school and preparing for my first collegiate baseball season in the Spring.

The Spring was much better because I didn't have enough time to complain about my life or travel home. My schedule forced me to stay up north and prepare. As February approached (that's when the college baseball season starts), I was in the best physical shape of my life and vying for getting significant innings as a freshman pitcher, which doesn't happen often. In week 4, I had thrown three scoreless innings out of the bullpen at University of Nevada, Reno and from that point on I was put into the starting rotation. My complaining had officially taken a back seat to my success. Unfortunately, it would only last two months.

During my last start of my freshman year at UOP in May of 2006, I felt uncomfortable during warm ups. I was not a big kid and I had thrown a lot of pitches throughout that season. My body had apparently broken down and was ready for a break. As I was warming up in the 9th inning trying to finish the game, I felt a sharp pain at the top of my throwing shoulder. It felt like someone was sticking a knife in my arm every time I released the ball. I battled through the inning and proceeded to put some ice on it after the game.

After the season, I went back to San Diego to participate in a Summer Collegiate League. I traveled home to play for the

San Diego Mavericks and would only have three outings. My body felt great, but I was still having a sharp pain in my shoulder when I would throw the ball. After talking to my college coaches, I was told to go get an MRI. I was nervous, but felt like I was invincible and this was probably something minor. After getting the arthrogram results from the doctor, I was shocked. My labrum had torn off the humeral head in my pitching arm. This is a significant pitching injury that I would find is very difficult to come back from. I was still only a 19-year old kid that didn't understand the extent of this injury. I thought I was still going to be fine and achieve my goal of playing professional baseball a few years down the road.

The next two years of my life were not easy to get through. I had a terrible outlook on everything because the most important thing to me in this world was ripped away, baseball. We all have goals or dreams as kids; at that time, I remember thinking about all of the effort I had put into being the best ball player I could be; then, at the blink of an eye, my arm would never feel the same. For some odd reason, I thought I would feel better about my situation if others felt bad for me. I wanted people to constantly check on me and ask if I was okay. Positivity was slowly being drained out of me. I rehabbed over the next 6 months and tried to make a comeback but was unsuccessful. My doctor then recommended that I get the surgery to staple everything back into place. This took another year of rehab in which I was not excited about. My grades dropped, my relationships became more toxic because I was negative on a daily basis. I didn't work my hardest in anything that I did. I came back again for my junior season at UOP and it was rough. Our team was terrible and I did not help the cause. The second half of my freshman year people looked up to me and I considered myself a team leader, at this point I was bringing everyone around me down.

I spent my days complaining about the pain in my arm and I slowly began to realize that my baseball career may be coming to an end. My dream of making it to the Major Leagues was fading and it physically and mentally destroyed me. I had completely wasted two years of my life because negativity and complaining were my most prevalent traits.

I was in the dumps and needed something positive in my life. The Summer going into my senior year at UOP was a turning point. I went to play Summer ball in McKinney, Texas where one of my good friends and college roommate Joe Oliveira had played the previous two Summers. He was expecting to get drafted that year, so I went out to Texas with a couple other UOP teammates. I was enjoying my time in this new atmosphere and had a great host family that treated me like a son. Cary and Tracy Linck along with their kids Carter and Abigail immediately made me feel like one of the family. About three weeks in, Joe didn't get taken in the MLB draft and decided he would come back for his senior year at UOP. He also decided to come back to McKinney for another Summer.

The past 2 years had seemed like 10 and the negativity that I had let take over my life made me feel as though that was my new normal. However, as quickly as things can go bad, there was a different vibe during that Summer. I started to catch some breaks in life. I had a great group of coaches that really helped me get my confidence on the mound back. Once again, just like my high school years, I was surrounded by confident people that pushed me. We had a couple of future big leaguers (Jimmy Nelson & Mike Bolsinger) on the team that I worked out with. I had to be the best version of myself to keep up with the guys on my team. As I started to have some success, baseball became fun again. My arm still wasn't feeling great, but I was getting outs. The mental side of my life was becoming a bigger and more important aspect of my everyday life.

I read the book *Mind Gym* over the Summer and it opened up my eyes. This is a great read for anyone looking to get a mental edge. I found ways to overcome my discomfort and mentally prepare myself for my pitching performances. This book enabled me to find ways to prepare my mind and not worry about the arm pain.   I was still in pain whenever I threw the ball, but now I had a mental edge. I began training my brain that what I was feeling in my arm was normal. I was never going to feel the same again due to the surgery, so I had to find a way to minimize the discomfort. Telling myself that what I was feeling in my arm was normal, helped me overcome that feeling of pain. *Mind Gym* helped me through a lot of my issues from a mental standpoint and put me on the right path towards mental toughness. This new edge led to more happiness in my life as well. The Summer of 2008 was coming to an end and I was back on the right track mentally; less complaining and more competing.

The first week back at school for my senior year of college and I felt like a new person. I was ready to leave it all out on the field, in the classroom, and in every other aspect of my life. My coach, Ed Sprague, had meetings with us the first week we got back to campus to catch up and see how the Summer was. I remember going in there with a plan. I was going to lay out all of my goals for myself and the team that year. I wanted to take back my leadership role by doing things right. After the past couple years, I know that a lot of trust was lost due to my work ethic, poor performance, and negative attitude.

It was early September when I walked into Coach Sprague's office and told him a few things. By this point in my career, I knew how to press Coach Sprague's competitive buttons to fire him up. We had some small talk to start, then we got into the nuts and bolts about the past. I told him that I am over the past and ready to move on.

Here were my personal goals:
1) Throw 100 innings in the Spring
2) Play CF or 1B if I wasn't on the mound
3) Do things to the best of my ability and set a standard for our team's work ethic
4) Do not complain about arm discomfort

I also had goals that I didn't mention that had to do with happiness, effort in the classroom, and mental training. I had all of my personal goals set; but my main goal was to be a great teammate and enjoy my final year. Sometimes things just happen, but most of the time things happen because we *make* them happen. I am proud to say that I worked my ass off my senior year of college in all aspects of my life. I got straight A's in the first semester which hadn't happened in my entire life. Our team didn't have a great year from a win/loss perspective, but other teams hated playing us. We were relentless workers and   never   quit.

There was one game in particular that I want to bring up that I am particularly proud of my teammates and coaches for. We were playing at the University of California, Riverside, who was especially talented that year. I did not have my best stuff that day on the mound, but battled. Sprague had the bullpen warming up each of the first three innings because I kept getting into trouble. If I would have been in a situation like this my sophomore or junior year, I would have told Coach Sprague to take me out because my arm hurt and I wouldn't give up 10 runs.   Instead, I just kept throwing the ball with as much competitiveness as I could muster up, and before you knew it, I was working into the 9th inning.   I had great teammates that instilled positivity and confidence in me every time I toed the pitching rubber. We were down 5-2 heading into the last inning when one of the best closers in the country was coming out from the bullpen. For those that don't know who Joe Kelly is, he throws 100mph and won a World Series with the Boston Red Sox during the 2018 season. He was frightening back in college and that night he was throwing hard. Our team always had confidence in our offensive ability. Instead of telling ourselves we were screwed because Joe Kelly was in, we stepped up to the challenge and went into the 9th with the thought that we can score some runs. In the top half of the 9th, we proceeded to score 7 runs (6 off of Kelly) and took a huge lead. I went out for the bottom of the 9th and finished the game on the mound. That was such a memorable moment because we knew how great of a team they were and how great of a pitcher Kelly was, but our brains had been trained to compete until the end and we knew how good of an offensive team we were. The ability in the opposing dugout didn't matter, we put our heads down and controlled what we could without worrying about the outcome.

My senior year of college I felt the transition of 'Joey the Boy' turning into 'Joey the Man'. I had a great support system of coaches, family, and friends that helped me commit to the changes I wanted to make in my life; mainly, the idea that *complaining about problems that arise in one's life does not make those problems go away.* I devoted part of my days to working on mental training so I could re-wire my brain to think a different way than I had before. I was more conscious of my thoughts. It was one of the best years of my life and I am glad that my teammates and coaches stuck with me during the rough times because it all led to a better version of me.

Negativity can set in any time we run into adversity. Staying positive and limiting complaining from our daily lives takes some hard work and mental training, but it will definitely help. I truly believe that it was not a coincidence during the Summer of 2008 that once I made the conscious thought to complain less, I became a more positive and happy person. I don't think I could have made these changes alone. The people in my life that helped me (friends, teammates, coaches, and family) deserve the credit for my transformation.

P.S. I finished the season with 99 innings (my goal was 100) which still eats me up to this day.

Chapter 8: Reacher vs. Settler

"Every good relationship has a reacher and a settler."

"Exactly. One person reaches for someone out of their league the other person settles for someone below theirs."

I learned about the Reacher vs. Settler analogy while watching the television show, *How I Met Your Mother*. Life is filled with reachers and settlers. We all have people in our lives that we are thinking of right now, and that's okay. As I will describe, reachers and settlers don't simply come in the form of relationships.

Settlers are the type of people that are okay with staying put. They don't like to go beyond their comfort level to challenge themselves. Settlers are usually people that could do more in their life, but choose not to. Let me also say this; being a settler isn't always a bad thing. Some people are very content with their lives and *want* to be settlers. I have several friends that have great lives that I feel are in the settler category.

Most of my settler friends aren't the happiest people in the world. In my experience, settlers are more likely to complain about their situation and express reasons why they can't advance to the next level of their lives. They usually don't have as much drive or willpower as the next people I will discuss.

Settling can be thought of on a few levels; the main two that come to mind for me are relationships and work life. If you have a significant other that does not meet your made-up standards in regards to intelligence, personality, compatibility, or other traits that are important to you, that makes you a settler. If you have aspirations of having a great job where you make a lot of money and it is something that you love to do, don't settle for anything less. Why settle in life when you can reach?

Reachers are those that go beyond their comfort level to accomplish certain things in their lives. These are people that feel they deserve more than they probably should. They go after goals and try to do more with their personal and professional lives. Reachers can also be described as dreamers in some cases.

Reachers aren't always successful. They have ideas of what they'd like to accomplish but don't necessarily always get there. Risking failure is a big part of being a reacher, but failure does not keep a reacher down. "Failures, repeated failures, are finger posts on the road to achievement. One fails forward toward success." This C.S. Lewis quote discusses the importance of failure. Reachers have to accept loss or failure sometimes and pick themselves up again.

It is a tough life to live to be a reacher because you will have more disappointment than a settler. Many reachers who don't have that drive may end up in the settler category after a short period of time; but, some reachers turn up that thermostat and become doers in the long-run.

The best kind of reacher is the doer. This type of person doesn't just chase their goals, they make sure that they do everything in their power to achieve those goals. Of course, nobody in this world is successful 100% of the time, but doers continue to drive themselves towards success no matter what roadblocks might be ahead. A former NFL punter and now motivational speaker, Steve Weatherford, phrases this as "assaulting your goals." I love the concept.

Assaulting goals is more active than *attempting* them. The word itself, while negative in a lot of contexts, conjures up the notion of maximum effort. When you merely *attempt* to box your opponent, you might dance around and even leave the ring without throwing a punch. But when you *assault* a boxing opponent, you take control, you force the issue, and you go for the knockout. You act with assurance and confidence. Sure, you may end up swinging and missing and taking a right cross to the head – we all fail goals from time to time – but isn't it better to fail with your best punch than to lose because you were afraid to try? Doers don't complain about situations that might hinder them. Doers find ways to make the most out of whatever the big man upstairs throws in front of them and they relentlessly attack that obstacle.

People that want more need to work as hard as they can to achieve what they've set out for themselves. If you want to get into better shape, you have to go to the gym and get a diet plan that works for you; it isn't just going to happen. People that have the work ethic to put their minds to something and accomplish it are a rare breed. There isn't much competition at the top because most people don't want to squeeze the orange, they just want the juice. What I'm saying is, people want the rewards but don't want all of the hard work that comes with it. A champion would work as hard as they could in everything that they do in order to get there. For those that want to accomplish more in their lives, it takes a lot of hard work and sometimes a lot of failure to get to a certain level of satisfaction.

"Stare at your destination like an obsession." That is a quote from Dean Graziosi, a well-known real estate guru. If you want to get to certain landmarks in your life, you need to work like a mule to get there. I bring up the mule because they work until the work is done. They carry, plow, or do whatever else they have to and don't stop until it is completed. Once that job is done, they move on to the next.

Don't let anything take you off course that may lead to complaining and quitting. Find what you want and put all of your energy into making sure you don't fall short. People chase goals their entire lives, but very few of us achieve most of what we set out to do. Why set goals if we are going to be okay with falling short of those goals time and time again? If you want to be a doer, only one person can help you reach that goal.

One of my favorite analogies comes from Ed Mylett, who I've mentioned earlier in this book. He brings to light our internal thermostat. We all have a certain level of self-worth in our lives which he calls 75 degrees. He chooses 75 degrees because that is a standard temperature that most people can equate to comfort. If we have points in our lives where we take that thermostat to 80 or 85 degrees, our body will naturally cool us back to 75 at some point because that's where our mind *thinks* we belong. On the other side of the spectrum, if we are at 65 degrees, we will heat up to 75 to get back to our comfort level. As humans, we need to find ways to increase that internal thermostat to 76, then 77, then 78, and beyond. Self-worth is the root of happiness and success; therefore, we should do everything in our power to increase that thermostat throughout our lives.

Many people will sit at 75 degrees and complain about what is limiting them from getting to 80 or 85 degrees. Surround yourself with 85-degree people and you will find ways to bring yourself up to that level. An 85-degree person is someone that maintains their composure when adversity or stress levels rise. Michael Strahan, Ellen DeGeneres, Shaquille O'Neal, those are 85-degree people. They continue to have success and don't stop climbing the ladder because they truly believe that they don't have a ceiling. They are able to overcome obstacles and stay focused on their main goal. It does come with some work.

Changing your thermostat is an everyday battle with yourself. There are going to be many successful days that you need to enjoy; but there will also be days that are a struggle. We have all experienced times when we have worked towards something and failed. Those 65-degree days when we don't want to put in the work to get our internal thermostat back up to 75 degrees anymore because it's easier to just quit. That is why it is much easier to have people around you that are working towards the same goal of raising that temperature. You have to *believe* that you deserve to be at those higher levels in order to get there.

I have not always been a reacher, I used to settle in many aspects of my life. I've found through much trial and error that constantly reaching is a positive way to live. I have goals that I am always reaching for, but I will not allow myself to become a settler once again. Complaining about what's in my way will not get those stop signs out of my face. When I come to one of them, I will stop, take a breath, and continue on towards the path of success. This is a patient process, but if I can see my long-term goals with a telescope, they are within my reach. I may not get everything done tomorrow, but if I have a plan and positive people around me, there is time to assault those goals.

You are what you think you are. If you truly believe that you deserve more happiness, better relationships, more money, or whatever it is; train your brain and visualize yourself at those levels. Then *reach* for it. When you can wake up and know that you are good enough for that job, your brain will find ways to get you an interview. If you wake up and complain about how you aren't as qualified as the other candidates and it's a waste of time, you have no chance. Go out and get qualified. Take extra courses, get another degree, volunteer in that industry to learn the ropes. Don't settle for what you have if you're not happy. There is always a way to get an edge and turn up that thermostat, so reach out and turn that dial.

Chapter 9: Mentors

It is important to have people to look up to in life that can help guide you in whatever direction you'd like to go. Obviously, it is much more beneficial to have the same values as our role models. This enables you to have a path to follow with some clear direction.   Most people start their lives out with parents as mentors and as we get older we find people outside of our families that have those qualities that we are looking to perfect for ourselves.

The first mentor I will dive into is former Major League Baseball third baseman – and my college coach – Ed Sprague. I've known him since 2004, and while I love him personally, I would have to say he is more of a role model for me in the professional sense than on a personal level.   When I was recruited to play baseball at the University of the Pacific, I remember going on my official visit and having dinner with the coaching staff. Sprague was still only 4 years or so out of the MLB at that point and a well-known figure in the world of baseball. I never was the type to get overly excited when I met famous people or athletes, but for some reason on this night I was in awe. He carried such professionalism and confidence in his demeanor and it caught my attention.   He radiated importance and purpose, even in the way he walked into and out of the restaurant. I wanted to be like him.

After playing for Sprague for 4 years, we stayed in touch through my short yet difficult journey in the Minor Leagues and beyond as I began my life in the real world. Fortunately, we had such a good relationship, after a few years of working down in San Diego, he urged me to apply for – and subsequently hired me as his assistant at UOP. I was ready to have a career next to Ed, but after coaching with him for only one year, the school parted ways with him – and our entire staff. I immediately went into complaining mode. My roommates and I had a few too many cocktails the day that it happened and began firing verbal blows to each other about anything we could think of in life that was unfair. In hindsight, I realize that the more professional way that Sprague overcame this obstacle was much more constructive. It was frustrating for all of us, and it had to be worse for him in many ways, but watching him turn the situation from a negative into a positive was beneficial for me as an adult.

I spent most of the Summer at home in Stockton feeling sorry for myself and drinking. I brought my roommates down to my level after trapping them in my web of complaints. I remember vividly going into my exit meeting with the university. I had a plan of what I wanted to say (and it wasn't positive), but when I sat down at the table I remember a calm coming over me. What good is my negativity going to do? This university has brought me so much joy over the past decade; I can't bring hatred into my heart over one decision that they made. I consciously thought about verbally dismantling the administration; but I took a breath when I sat down and had a clean and positive discussion. This was a turning point for me. Consciously understanding what my brain is telling me and learning to step back in some situations is a difficult skill to master.

I never heard a peep of anger come out of Sprague although I'm sure he felt it at times. He landed a great job with the Oakland Athletics and continues to work his way up the MLB ladder. His transition from being let go at UOP to working in professional baseball allowed him to display the immense poise that likely got him these incredible opportunities to begin with. I have seen plenty of coaches get fired and leave their respective job kicking and screaming (which is exactly what I wanted to do); but complaining about his situation was not going to help in any way. Sprague simply put his head down and worked until someone hired him. It's taken me some time, but I have learned how to carry myself and can say with confidence that I went into UOP a boy and graduated a more mature man ready to take on the real world thanks to Coach Sprague.

My next mentor is not quite as famous as Ed Sprague, but was a complete rock star in the classroom. I have never been a very energetic person, but I know that carrying enthusiasm while I am coaching helps the players have more energy on the ball field. Mr. Fares was my English teacher at the University of San Diego High School in 2005, my senior year. I substitute taught for a while in my early years of coaching high school baseball, but I don't know what it's like to teach one subject for about 40 years. Mr. Fares always came to the classroom with more energy than the students. He was like a virus that passed on positivity and liveliness to the students in his class. We all have those teachers or subjects that we dread. Mr. Fares made English fun for a bunch of students that weren't motivated because it was our senior year and most of us already had been accepted to various colleges. He could have complained about the lack of work ethic or energy in the classroom – which most likely would not have been the recipe to make us work harder; instead, he acted and taught us in a way that *forced* us to care. He didn't do it by being a pushover either. He made us work hard, and he somehow made working hard desirable. He did a lot of things that had the opposite effect of what you would expect. Mr. Fares liked challenging us, sometimes yelling out instructions as though he were mad – before smiling and releasing a loud cackle. He kept us on our toes and instilled in us a new perspective.

One of my fondest memories of that English class was on a Friday towards the end of the school year. Most of the seniors are checked out and ready for the Summer at that point. My girlfriend at the time was and aid for the office and would occasionally walk into our class with a note that a someone needed to meet their counselor. At times, she would also bring in detention slips. As my buddy Ryan and his girlfriend were in the back of the classroom flirting, we all heard *Saturday Night's Alright for Fighting* by Elton John begin to blast throughout the classroom. As the walls were shaking, Mr. Fares began to flail his arms and moonwalk down the aisle to Ryan's seat where he proceeded to hand him a 2-hour Saturday detention. Although Ryan wasn't ecstatic, he took it like a champ. What used to be the worst punishment imaginable to a high schooler suddenly became an opportunity to step back and laugh at ourselves, knowing we could do better next time. He has been an inspiration for me throughout my life because I now understand that no matter what situation is ahead, if I attack it with perspective, passion, and positive energy I can enjoy whatever I do.

Mr. Fares also helped with my writing. I have always been okay, but he helped me get the most out of my creative side. We regularly wrote journals in his class in which he allowed us to open up and write about anything that was on our minds. It was freeing to get away from the X's and O's of the MLA format and let my brain wander into new territories. I am grateful that he was a big part of my learning process and that I was able to enjoy his English class throughout my senior year. The reason I mention this section about writing is because in Chapter 5 I discuss things that may help you when you feel the urge to complain. Writing became an integral part of my weekly routine. Writing my feelings and thoughts down in Mr. Fares' class enabled me to get those complaining notions out of my head.   Those days helped me keep a positive attitude even when they were sprinkled with negativity.

That passion and enthusiasm that Mr. Fares brought every day could have been used by me more effectively when I got a job at Point Loma Sportfishing one Summer. I was in college rehabbing my arm in San Diego and needed to get a job rather than mooch off of my parents for 2 ½ months. I had to be at the docks by 4:30am to beat the boats that were coming back from overnight trips. I had zero interest in fishing and everyone knew it.   My co-workers could see and feel my negativity when I unlocked the front doors. When customers would come to my window (which looked out at the gorgeous bay and boats) to ask me what the numbers of fish caught looked like the previous day I would answer with a smug look showing I did not care.

Luckily for me, my brother and sister worked there as well and were great employees.   If they hadn't been so awesome at everything, I'm sure my bosses would have fired me due to my poor attitude and terrible work ethic. They talked to me a few times about customers complaining to them about me. The main part of my job was answering phones and making reservations for all of the deep-sea fishing boats.   When customers would ask me questions that I did not have answers to, I would complain about my job and tell them I didn't know anything about fishing.

If only I was able to conjure my inner Mr. Fares at that time. Sometimes we don't really see these things until years down the road. Knowing what his teaching methods mean to me now, I look back and realize I could have done a lot of things differently. We all have these defining moments in our lives. Writing this book has helped me understand that I have more defining moments than I thought. I am continuing to learn from my past to help me prepare for the future and enjoy the present moment.

My next mentor ended up falling into my lap. I had never heard of motivational speaker Ed Mylett, even though he had graduated from the same university as me and even played baseball there back in the '90s. If it weren't for one of my players sending me a YouTube video of Mylett, I probably never would have known he existed.

Mylett was a person that wanted to help other people because he could. He seemed like he was the busiest person in the world; always on the road for charity events, speaking engagements, or just for a little family vacation. Baseball was a huge part of his life for many years, but an injury in college changed his future. Until he took a public speaking class at UOP during his last semester, he didn't realize that talking to others was something he was good at. He was actually frightened to speak and was known to be more of a reserved guy early in his life.

After college, he struggled with some odd jobs here and there and didn't know what he wanted to do. Living in a small place with no money and sneakily taking showers at the downstairs pool of his apartment complex to save on the water bill, Ed didn't know what his next steps were. Knowing his own potential, Mylett didn't complain about his situation, he embraced it and worked hard until he landed a job at World Financial Group. At WFG, Mylett began making an impact. He was extremely successful in his first few years and eventually took over the company. During his time at WFG, Mylett began to see that he could help others with his knowledge and communication skills. He started to set up speaking engagements with various companies to motivate employees and help them run more efficiently. I would consider Mylett to be more of a "pump you up" type of speaker. He has the ability to excite you about your job and future. I saw this first-hand when he spoke to our 2018-19 Pacific Tigers baseball team.

Before we met, I took an unorthodox route to getting ahold of Mylett. I was looking up some of his material on Instagram and decided I would send him a direct message. I remember thinking to myself, "This guy has more money than Will Smith. No way he gets back to me." In the message, I asked if he'd be interested in coming up to talk to our team. After a couple messages back and forth, he called me about a week later. This is a man that was named one of the wealthiest 50 people under the age of 50. He has a full plate with speaking engagements, his YouTube show, along with hundreds of other things. Two months after we had been talking about getting him up to campus, he showed up at UOP for the first time in 25 years. He got out of his rental car and there was an immediate aura of positivity around him. He didn't have to be there talking to our team (for free); but he felt a connection with our program and wanted to help out in any way.

Mylett has some inspirational and positive people on his YouTube show. He works hard to help people gain a better perspective of life...a happier one. Many of his guests are experts in their field or they are simply positive people. They are successful in their fields because they put in the work and don't let setbacks ruin their ultimate goals. A hunger for happiness pushes these people to limits they didn't know they had. Their willingness to drive themselves is inspirational and would help any person; whether you are already happy or find yourself complaining more than you would like. I've found that Mylett's words and shows are insightful. He has enough money to do whatever he wants, but he chooses to help millions of people around the world reach their potential.

My final mentor is someone that has been extremely close to me since birth. He is not as much of an 'in your face' mentor as someone like Ed Mylett, but this person has had a direct impact on my life. My Uncle Perry has been someone that I can look up to because he carries so much internal strength. He lived with and took care of my Nonna for several years. When he was diagnosed with cancer, my family was put into a tough spot. You remember the bad-ass Italian woman that took out the hornet's nest with a hockey stick? With Uncle Perry having to go through chemo and lose much of his strength, other family members were going to have to step up and help out.

Uncle Perry has been a "lead by example" mentor for me. I was able to communicate with him, but just watching his actions and behaviors while he was going through this time was beneficial for me. No matter how weak he felt, there was always enough strength for a smile. At times, it was difficult for him to get out of his seat; but he could still crack a joke about getting some spinach so he could feel as strong as Popeye. His positivity while he fought for his life was inspiring. He beat cancer twice and continues to live a happy life. I hope to never go through what he had to on two separate occasions.

After beating cancer twice, he was then diagnosed with a virus that doctors were a bit confused about. He woke up one day unable to move anything other than his head. He was taken to the hospital for testing. His myelin sheath had been deteriorating throughout his body inhibiting him from having the strength to move. Myelin sheaths are sleeves of fatty tissue that protect your nerve cells. These cells are part of your central nervous system, which carries messages back and forth between your brain and the rest of your body. He is still fighting every day in hopes of gaining that strength back throughout his body. This has been yet another difficult process for him, but his lack of complaining and positive support from family and friends have led to great strides with his strength. Although it is a difficult time, the learning and reflection that he and our family have gone through is an experience that has made us stronger.

I have learned many life lessons from Uncle Perry's various health difficulties. The understanding that life is a precious commodity is the most valuable of them. We can't waste our lives away with negativity and pessimism. Strive for happiness and learn how to drive through those barriers that are constantly put up in our daily lives.

Seeking out mentors that you respect and/or want to model yourself after is important. You can still be yourself, and you should, but having people that obtain the traits that you'd like to mold into your life can be highly beneficial. I have lots of mentors, I just decided to pick out four because they all play such a different role in my life. Ed Sprague has been more of a professionalism role model to me. Mr. Fares conveys the energy that I look to bring to work every day. Ed Mylett has the drive and willingness to help. Uncle Perry has led by example. The willingness to help should be the easiest, but I have found it to be the most challenging because I need to set aside time for others. It is not always on the forefront of my mind and difficult with a busy work schedule, but when I do help out a worthy cause financially or at a volunteer capacity, my self-worth goes through the roof. None of us are perfect, but if we strive for perfection in all aspects of life we have the chance of settling for greatness.

Chapter 10: Someone to Love

There are countless ways people find love with another person. Finding someone to love can be integral in loving yourself. It can be any kind of love, mine happened to be romantic. I have been fortunate throughout my life and have had some great learning experiences from prior relationships and friendships. I finally ran into Julie while working at UOP for my first stint in 2014.

Everything wasn't perfect the first year and a half of our relationship. We were both still getting over our past significant others, and in many ways our time together was just an escape. We would watch movies at her place. We would get drinks together with our roommates. It was fun enough at the beginning, but when she mentioned that she wanted to move to San Diego after getting her Master's degree, I figured the fun was up.

We decided from the get go that we would not do long distance, so when she got the job in San Diego, we mutually decided to end things. That part was sad enough for most people to complain. But my complaints couldn't help what happened one month later, because this was the same summer that Ed Sprague and our staff were fired at UOP. Now I was alone in Stockton, CA without a job, without an escape, and without someone to love. My happiness began to decrease and my complaining skyrocketed.

As stated earlier, at the end of the Summer, I was offered the volunteer coaching job at San Diego State. I knew what lied ahead; 10-12 hours of work every day to make just enough to pay my bills. I wasn't happy, but Julie was down there. After we had broken up a few months earlier, she had decided that she didn't want anything to do with me. I spent endless hours moping around and pouring my heart out to my family about my terrible situation (which I'm sure they did not enjoy). The Summer of 2015 was filled with more complaining than any other point in my life. I had lost a great girl, my dream job, and most of my self-confidence. There was a lot to complain about.

With persistence, and maybe a few text messages and calls every day, I finally got Julie to agree to meet me for frozen yogurt one night. Refusing to complain, I finally found a way to go after what I wanted in a self-assured way. I joke that it was "borderline stalker," but once I let go of negativity, she could feel that I was being sincere. Yogurt led to another date, and I kept testing her limits showing her that I was ready to do whatever was necessary for the relationship to move forward.

I am guessing that it wasn't a coincidence that once Julie and I began to get serious again, my complaining drastically subsided. My lack of complaining and the confidence I had in the quest for re-wooing Julie saved me from falling off the deep end into a complaint-filled world. I was unhappy with my living and work situations, but she was the best thing in my life. I mentioned before, I don't know how she put up with me, but she was the light that kept me battling through tough days. Knowing that after work I was going to be able to spend time with her uplifted me and minimized the negativity. I still found ways to complain about my job at San Diego State that first year I was there, but I was in a better place socially.

After my first year at San Diego State, things were going extremely well with Julie and we decided to move in together. My personal life began to get better and more enjoyable. Things were going so well in the relationship that my attitude towards work got better as well. Julie's positivity and ability to make me happy slowly altered my complaining lifestyle to one of determination and self-motivation. I started getting up earlier in the mornings to work out and do some work in the office before anyone got there. I began reaching out to more coaches to catch up on life so I would have some feelers out there for the following Summer in case any jobs opened up. The love that Julie has given me has changed me into a much happier person.

It was a whirlwind of emotions in July and August of 2017. About a week after I had asked Julie to marry and she accepted, I received a job offer back up at UOP from Ryan Garko. Julie made the decision to move back up to Stockton with me and start our lives together. Once again, things were getting better and I was happier. We have enjoyed marriage and continue to find happiness in the small things that we are lucky to do together.

There are two ways you can go about fixing the complaining problem in your life:

    1) You wait for good things to start happening

    2) You change your mindset, be aware of your thoughts, and force good things to start happening

We have all had both of these situations arise in our lives. But from my experiences, route 2 is a much better way to *make* things happen. Control your destiny and put some hard work into a mindset change that will gradually turn that negativity into positivity.

Complaining is a toxic problem that plagues the lives of so many around the world. There are many ways to limit your complaining, but it doesn't just happen. It takes a mindset adjustment or even sometimes it can take an entire personality adjustment to make these important changes in your life. Use the ideas and information in this book to defeat the positivity-sucking disease. Surround yourself with happy, motivated people and search for someone that you can find love and joy with. We weren't put on this Earth to be negative and spend our lives dragging others down with our complaints; so, make a change and be a ray of light in someone else's life with your positivity.

<u>Chapter 11: Quotes</u>

I wanted to finish this book with some quotes that I've found or created over the past several years. I am a huge fan of quotes and use them daily as inspiration. I don't just use them for myself either, I spread them around to friends, family, and most notably, my players. Every week I put a quote on their schedule. Usually these quotes have something to do with happiness, breathing, work ethic, or I'll just mix in a comedic quote to get a rise out of them in some cases. Words are powerful and if you start your day thinking of something you're grateful for along with a motivational quote, you are going to have those positivity endorphins going wild first thing in the morning.

On the next few pages you will find 31 quotes. This can be a great starting point for you to make a change if you feel the need. Over the next month, read one of these quotes every morning and think of something that you are grateful for. Start your day off on the right foot and make a change! After the month is up, I hope you take the initiative to veer away from the path of complaints and find yourself on the highway towards happiness.

"You get out of life what you accept." –Ed Mylett

"The way you do one thing is the way you do everything."
–Ed Mylett

"Gratitude is the wine for the soul. Go on. Get drunk." –Rumi

"Gratitude and complaining cannot co-exist simultaneously. You must choose the one that best serves you." –Hal Elrod

"Instead of complaining that the rose bush is full of thorns, be happy the thorn bush has roses." –Proverb

"Either you run the day or the day runs you." –Jim Rohn

"Complaining shows that you are not in control of the situation." –Joey Centanni

"A flower does not think about competing with the flower next to it. It just blooms." –Zen Shin

"We may encounter many defeats but we must not be defeated." –Maya Angelou

"If you don't like something, change it. If you can't change it, change your attitude. Don't complain." –Maya Angelou

"If you want to conquer the anxiety of life, live in the moment, live in the breath." –Amit Ray

"The true test of a man's character is what he does when no one is watching." –John Wooden

"Champions never complain, they are too busy getting better." –John Wooden

"When you complain, you make yourself a victim. Leave the situation, change the situation, or accept it. All else is madness." –Eckhart Tolle

"Complaining is one of the ego's favorite strategies for strengthening itself." –Eckhart Tolle

"People won't have time for you if you are always angry and complaining." –Stephen Hawking

"If you practice gratitude a little, your life will change a little. If you practice gratitude a lot every day, your life will change dramatically and in ways that you can hardly imagine."
–Rhonda Byrne

"Like crying wolf, if you keep looking for sympathy as a justification for your actions, you will someday be left standing alone when you really need help." –Criss Jami

"We can throw stones, complain about them, stumble on them, climb over them, or build with them." –William Arthur Ward

"It is a rare person who, when his cup frequently runs over, can thank God instead of complaining about the limited size of his mug!" –Bob Russell

"If you have time to whine and complain about something then you have the time to do something about it."
–Anthony D'Angelo

"Don't cry because it's over, smile because it happened."
–Dr. Seuss

"You can never complain your way to a fulfilling life."
–Edmond Mbiaka

"Man spends his life in reasoning on the past, in complaining of the present, in fearing the future." –Antoine Rivarol

"Constant complaint is the poorest sort of pay for all the comforts we enjoy." –Benjamin Franklin

"When life gives you lemons, make lemonade and sell it to all of those who get thirsty from complaining." –Napolean Hill

"Do not listen to those who weep and complain, for their disease is contagious." –Og Mandino

"Have an attitude of gratitude and you will have more to be grateful for; have a complaining spirit and you will attract more to complain about." –Zig Ziglar

"Gratitude turns what we have into enough." –Melody Beattie

"Life is 10% what happens to you and 90% how you react to it." –Charles R. Swindoll

"It is better to light one small candle of gratitude than to curse the darkness." –Confucius

Sources

Belic, Roko, director. *Happy. IMDb*, 2013,
    www.imdb.com/title/tt1613092/.

Bergland, Christopher. "Cortisol: Why the 'Stress Hormone' Is
    Public Enemy No. 1." *Psychology Today*, Sussex
    Publishers, 2013, www.psychologytoday.com/us/blog/the-
    athletes-way/201301/cortisol-why-the-stress-hormone-is-
    public-enemy-no-1.

Bradberry, Travis. "Emotional Intelligence (EQ): The Premier
    Provider - Tests, Training, Certification, and
    Coaching." *TalentSmart*,
    www.talentsmart.com/articles/How-Complaining-Rewires-
    Your-Brain-for-Negativity-2147446676-p-1.html.

Dweck, Carol. *Mindset*. Robinson, 2017.

Mack, Gary, and David Casstevens. *Mind Gym: An Athlete's
    Guide to Inner Excellence*. Contemporary Books, 2001.

Marham, Laura. "The Average Person Complains 30 Times a
    Day...Would You like to Stop?" *Active Family Magazine*,
    31 Dec. 2014, www.activefamilymag.com/average-person-
    complains-30-times-day-like-stop/.

Meah, Asad. "35 Inspirational Quotes To Stop You From
    Complaining." *Awaken The Greatness Within*, 14 Jan.
    2018, awakenthegreatnesswithin.com/35-inspirational-
    quotes-to-stop-you-from-complaining/.

Mercola, Joseph. "Neuroplasticity Studies Reveal Your Brain's
    Amazing Malleability." *Mercola.com*, 15 Jan. 2015,

articles.mercola.com/sites/articles/archive/2015/01/15/neur
oplasticity-brain-health.aspx.

"NewswireToday Leading Press Releases & Newswire
Distribution Service." *NewswireToday*, Boom! Dialogue
Ltd., 2010, www.newswiretoday.com/news/76151/New-
Survey-Reveals-Average-Brit-Has-27-Conversations-
Every-Day/.

Parton, Steven. "Steven Parton." *Curious Apes*, 7 Nov. 2017,
www.curiousapes.com/the-science-of-happiness-why-
complaining-is-literally-killing-you/.

Seligman, Martin. "Martin Seligman." *Pursuit of Happiness*,
www.pursuit-of-happiness.org/history-of-
happiness/martin-seligman-psychology/.

Thomas, Andrew. "7 Scientific Ways to Stop Complaining and
Enjoy a Happier Life." *Inc.com*, Inc., 30 Jan. 2017,
www.inc.com/andrew-thomas/7-ways-to-stop-
complaining-and-feel-happier-backed-by-science.html.

Vozza, Stephanie. "Why Complaining May Be Dangerous To
Your Health." *Fast Company*, Fast Company, 12 Jan. 2015,
www.fastcompany.com/3040672/why-complaining-may-be-
dangerous-to-your-health.